Can Martha Have a Mary Christmas?

Can Martha Have a Mary Christmas?

Untangling Expectations and Truly Experiencing Jesus

Brenda Poinsett

new
hope
PUBLISHERS

Birmingham, Alabama

New Hope® Publishers
P. O. Box 12065
Birmingham, AL 35202-2065
www.newhopepublishers.com

Library of Congress Cataloging-in-Publication Data
Poinsett, Brenda.
Can Martha have a Mary Christmas? : untangling expectations and truly experiencing Jesus / Brenda Poinsett.
p. cm.
ISBN 1-56309-931-4 (pbk.)
1.   Women-Religious life. 2. Christmas. I. Title.
BV4527.P63 2005
248.8'43—dc22
2005011312

Unless otherwise indicated, all Scripture quotations in this publication are from the Good News Translation—Second Edition Copyright © 1992 by American Bible Society. Used by Permission.

Scripture quotations marked (HCSB) are taken from the Holman Christian Standard Bible © copyright 2000 by Holman Bible Publishers. Used by permission.

Scripture quotations marked (NIV) are taken from the HOLY BIBLE, NEW INTERNATIONAL VERSION®. NIV®. Copyright©1973, 1978, 1984 by International Bible Society. Used by permission of Zondervan. All rights reserved.

Scripture quotations marked (NASB) are taken from the New American Standard Bible®, Copyright © 1960, 1962, 1963, 1968, 1971, 1972, 1973, 1975, 1977, 1995 by The Lockman Foundation. Used by permission.

Scripture quotations marked (Williams) are taken from the *Williams New Testament, The New Testament in the Language of the People*, by Charles B. Williams. Copyright © 1937, 1966, 1986 by Holman Bible Publishers. Used by permission.

Scripture quotations marked (KJV) are taken from The Holy Bible, King James Version.

ISBN: 1-56309-931-4

N054117 • 1005 • 5M1

To Donna Williams,

who shares my interest

in celebrating with meaning

contents

acknowlegments

As a wife and mother, I was earnest about making Jesus the focus of our Christmas celebrations. The results were so rewarding that I wanted to share with others how they could have a simple, meaningful Christmas—one in which they could truly experience Jesus. To do this, I started offering workshops, but I had difficulty finding a title that would communicate exactly what I wanted to share. This is where my friend Donna Williams came to the rescue. She suggested the title, "Can Martha Have a 'Mary' Christmas?" That was it! When using that title, nothing else needed to be said. Women instinctively knew what the workshop would be about.

One of those women was Rebecca England, editor at New Hope. In checking out my website for my earlier book with New Hope, *She Walked With Jesus*, Rebecca spotted the workshop title "Can Martha Have a 'Mary' Christmas?" She said, "This sounds like a book in the making." And now it is a book, so I am very grateful to Donna and Rebecca. Although the content was present in my workshops, files, and heart, there wouldn't have been this book without these two women.

In addition to Rebecca, I'm thankful to the rest of the New Hope staff for their hard work and professionalism in bringing about a product that will help many women, and one I'm proud of. Not all publishers are sensitive to an author's feelings and opinions. I'm glad to say that the staff at New Hope are, and I'm especially grateful to Tara Miller, who listened to my concerns and considered my input.

I'm thankful, too, for the people who were a part of the many meaningful Christmases I've experienced. I am especially thankful for my family of Bob, Jim, Joel, Eri, Ben, and Christophe, my mother, Lorene Spires, and friends and acquaintances who attended our Christmas gatherings. I trust I have the details right about all of our interactions. If I haven't, please forgive me. Memory is durable, but not always accurate! When two or more people look back at the original scene, they don't always agree on what happened. I'll admit in an instance or two, I wasn't sure of a name, so I gave the persons names. If you read this book and identify yourself, I hope you will contact me.

Although Bob lived the experiences with me, I appreciate his willingness to read and to critique the manuscript, to serve as a sounding board, and to pray for me. I also appreciate my friends Pat McAlister and Jane Goodwin. Pat read and critiqued a chapter, and Jane gave me some valuable feedback via email.

I am appreciative of the people who prayed for me as I wrote this book: Barbara Popp, Lorraine Powers, Vivian McCaughan, Chris Dulworth, Michelle Magruder, Linda Magruder, Jan Turner, Barbara Williams, and Jim Poinsett. There may have been others who prayed and who didn't tell me. That happens with prayer. We reap the benefits even though we don't always know when someone is praying. I am touched and humbled by their efforts and by the thoughtfulness of all those mentioned here. I am a blessed woman, and I pray you will be blessed as you read this book.

THE MOST
*M*ARTHA TIME
OF THE YEAR

I sn't it interesting how a Biblical name becomes associated with a type of person?

Refer to a person as a Judas, and we know you mean he's a traitor.

Say "She's nothing but a Jezebel" and we understand you mean she is evil.

Call a woman a Martha, and busyness automatically registers on the brain.

The association of Martha with busyness goes back to an incident in Jesus' life. Martha, a resident of Bethany of Judea, invited Jesus of Galilee to her home, which she shared with her sister Mary and her brother Lazarus (Luke 10:38–42). Martha responded as I would if I had a guest in my home. I would have to offer him something to eat! I'm a Martha, and I come from a long line of Marthas, and we wouldn't think of entertaining guests without feeding them!

Martha scurried around fixing a meal for Jesus, making sure He was comfortable. She wanted everything to be just right for Him so He would be refreshed when He continued on His journey. Her invitation provided an opportunity for Mary—possibly Lazarus, too—to listen to Jesus. If His disciples were with Him—and they usually were—then her arms and her heart would have reached out to them, too. We Marthas are just that way. We look after people and the details of life. We entertain, cook, clean, and organize. We keep families functioning, households running, offices organized, and churches humming. I take pride in being a Martha; I like to think we keep the world turning.

Not all women are Marthas, but even women who aren't generally become Marthas at Christmas. How else would Christmas get done if it weren't for us?

A Woman's Holiday

We plan the menus and buy and prepare most of the food. We shop and shop for gifts and spend hours wrapping them. We buy and send the majority of greeting cards. We decorate our houses—first we clean them! We make our workplaces festive, too. We host parties, luncheons, open houses, and family dinners.

In the process, it is not unusual for us to become like Martha of Bethany in another way. In her earnestness of wanting Jesus' visit to go well, she became "worried and upset about many things" (Luke 10:41 HCSB).

The "many things" part happens easily enough because we have an eye for details. Women are constantly taking in and responding to what's going on around us. We can't help but note things that need attention—or correcting! We see things that others may easily overlook or never even see, such as an uneven tablecloth, fingerprints on the refrigerator, and unmatched bathroom towels.

But it is not the details alone that cause us to become worried and upset; we also want to please others. It's almost as if there is a "people-pleaser" gene nestled in our brains right behind that eye for details. We want to make others happy, so we get concerned and anxious, wondering if others are having a good time, if they liked what we prepared, or if they will be pleased with our gifts.

Christmas turns women into Marthas, but it doesn't have the same effect on men. To men who mostly wait until after December 18 to do their Christmas shopping, a gift is a gift. A woman, though, will shop and shop until she finds the right gift—and at the best price! A man who needs a gift for his wife, say a blouse, will go to a store, find the blouse rack, locate a blouse in her size, buy it, and be done with shopping. Does it matter that there could be a prettier blouse at a better price at another store? Not to him, but it does to her when she's buying!

Likewise, to most men, a meal is a meal. Does it matter whether family members converse during Christmas dinner after all the turkey and dressing are outstanding? Does it matter if the globes of the light fixture over the dining table haven't been washed in the last six months? He asks, "Who is going to notice they are dusty?" You sigh heavily as you think of the Marthas who will be present; they will notice and, more importantly, *you* will know. Located right next to the "people-pleaser" gene is a "must-do-it-right" gene.

Dreaming of a Right Christmas

Women have many different ways of celebrating, but however they choose to celebrate, they want to "do it right." In her mind, a woman has a picture of what an ideal Christmas should be. She works hard trying to make her real Christmas match her ideal. Most men don't seem to have this kind of internal standard to please. Christmas is Christmas is Christmas. It doesn't matter to men whether the fruit salad is served in an exquisite glass dish or a margarine tub. Neither do men care if the decorations reflect a certain theme or are color-coordinated.

Perhaps I am extra sensitive to the differences between the way women and men respond to Christmas because I live with *Scrooge*. My husband Bob isn't stingy like the character from Charles Dickens's *A Christmas Carol*, but he remains detached from Christmas. Bob himself describes his response to Christmas as "an uninvolved participant." Bob goes through the motions of observing the holiday, but he seldom gets involved.

When our family plans a tree decorating party, Ben will make the brownies, Jim will fix hot apple cider, I will open the boxes of Christmas ornaments while humming *Gather Around the Christmas Tree,* and Joel will untangle the strings of lights. Bob will hang an ornament or two on the tree, but before we know it, he's in another room reading a magazine.

"Hey, Dad, come and join us?" Ben will yell. Bob stays with his magazine.

Joel will say, "Come on, Dad. It's Christmas." With more urging, Bob might venture back into the family room long enough to hang another ornament or straighten the tree if it has tilted, but soon he's back to his magazine.

Bob doesn't get his feelings wrapped up in Christmas the way I do. Bob chooses not to be involved, and bless his heart, he doesn't even appreciate the fact that he has a choice. Women do not have a choice. Participating in Christmas goes with being a woman.

Whether you work in an office, in a factory, in a retail store, or at home, whether you are single or married, young or old, you are expected to see that Christmas happens. And this is in addition to looking after all your regular responsibilities! No wonder the Christmas season becomes the most Martha time of the year.

Busy Yet . . .

Not having a choice is all right with some women because Christmas is their time to shine. They excel at decorating, gift giving, and entertaining. Some women, though, feel burdened by always having to be responsible for Christmas. They get a tad resentful that the relatives assume Christmas dinner will always be at their house or that the office workers count on them to coordinate the Christmas potluck. Some get just plain tired and frazzled from all they have to do. They question if Christmas preparation is worth all their effort; there doesn't seem to be much return on their investment. Some women worry so much about Christmas that they have a hard time turning off that "must do it right" gene. In mid-January, they send out the Christmas cards they didn't have time to send in December. Christmas cards are a part of a *right* Christmas, so it must be done.

No wonder the thoughts, feelings, and expectations women have about Christmas get all tangled up. One December day you can be happily baking cookies and the next day you are thinking, "I'll be glad when Christmas is over." One moment you take a few minutes out to sit quietly listening to Christmas carols and you think, "Christmas is so special." An hour later, though, you may be thinking, "The pressure is incredible. Will I ever have everything ready?"

And lying just below the surface of all these frustrations and worries is a haunting sense that there ought to be something more. After all, it's Jesus' birthday. Somewhere in the celebration, shouldn't we experience something spiritual? Somewhere amid the hustle and bustle, shouldn't we experience Jesus the way Martha's sister Mary did?

Mary planted herself near Jesus, listened to what He had to say, learned from Him, and interacted with Him. Now that's something I want to experience! Do you?

But how can a Martha who sees so much that needs to be done, who wants to please people, and who wants to do Christmas right, have a "Mary" Christmas? Is it even possible?

I believe it is, but it takes some untangling of our thoughts, feelings, and expectations, and looking for ways to connect with Jesus. When Joel untangles our lights, he stretches them out strand by strand until they cover the family room floor where he can get a good look. He works all the kinks out of the cords, and then he plugs them in. Some of last year's lights still glow. Others don't, and Joel replaces those before he put the lights on the tree.

Untangling Christmas tree lights requires space—something Marthas don't have much of in December. With this book, we can grab some space here and there to reflect. When we do, we will get out some of the kinks. We will be able to see lights from past Christmases twinkling clear and bright. We are doing some things right! And we'll see where new lights can be turned on. We will see ways we can make changes that will enable us to have a "Mary" Christmas.

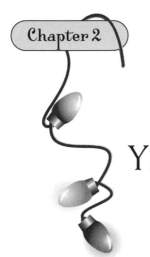

Chapter 2

YES, *M*ARTHA, THERE IS A REAL JESUS

Where do our dreams begin? Where do our aspirations originate? What prompts the swelling in our minds of images we want to see come to reality?

When Irving Berlin wrote "I'm Dreaming of a White Christmas," he was in California. The sun was shining, the grass was green, and palm trees swayed in the breeze. Weather-wise, it was a perfect day, and yet he longed for snow—a white Christmas like he had known in his past.

Our past may have a lot to do with the kind of Christmas we want as adults. The way your mother made dressing, the traditions you celebrated as a family, the fun you had being in the church play, the warmth of a cup of hot chocolate, the glow of Christmas lights, the quiet reflection of Christmas Eve Vespers, or opening a surprise gift that just suited you.

Mental images kaleidoscope together and take shape as a Christmas dream. The dream forms, plants itself in our heads, and becomes a motivator.

When I grow up, I will...

If I get married, I'm going to...

When I have a home of my own, I will...

When we have children, I want to...

When I'm making more money, then I will...

While my dream to have a "Mary" Christmas may appear as an escape wish from so many Martha responsibilities, its roots go deeper than that. I can trace the origin back to a cold January day when I was eight years old. I was walking back to school with some classmates after Christmas vacation. One of them asked, "What did Santa Claus bring you for Christmas?"

"Santa brought me a doll," I answered. "What did he bring you?"

Before she could answer, a third little girl spouted, "Santa Claus didn't bring you anything."

"Yes, he did," we insisted.

"Santa Claus didn't bring you anything because there is no Santa. Don't you know that, silly?"

There's probably not an eight-year-old alive now that believes in Santa Claus, but I did. My mind began working furiously trying to sort out the truth. *Santa Claus? Not real? Dear wonderful Santa has to be real.*

I had to admit I had been suspicious. How could Santa get down narrow chimneys with his round belly? How did he get in to homes without fireplaces? Why were toys collected for poor children if Santa visited *all* the boys and girls in the world? Why did some children get more than others?

Suddenly I had a sinking feeling that my classmate was right. *There was no real Santa Claus.*

I was disappointed and angry. I thought, "The next thing they (those adults who conspire against children) will tell us is that there is no baby Jesus, either." If one was a made-up person, then the other one probably was, too.

I didn't want to be caught unaware again, so I began observing adults to see if the baby Jesus story was also a legend. Like Virginia, the famous little girl who wrote to a newspaper to see if there was a Santa Claus, I wanted to know if Jesus was real. I didn't write to a newspaper, but I watched and listened, especially at church. If Jesus wasn't real, then surely there would be clues. Some adult would slip with the evidence. As carefully as I listened, I didn't pick up any clues. Everybody at church talked and acted as if Jesus were real.

Our pastor said, "Jesus forgives sin, and everyone sins, including boys and girls." I recognized *that* as truth! I knew that I had done wrong things. The pastor encouraged us to confess our sins to Jesus and proclaim faith in Him in front of the church. The thought of that scared me, but eventually my desire for forgiveness overcame my fears. I asked for forgiveness and confessed my belief in Jesus.

Then I experienced something that has been the hallmark of my relationship with Jesus ever since: Jesus responded. He forgave my sins. One has to be real to respond!

As our relationship developed, Jesus continued to respond. I could count on a good conversation with Him any time. He responded to my concerns with understanding and guidance. He helped me be a good student and a good daughter. Sometimes when I was lonely and thought no one liked me, He assured me that He loved me. He was an especially good confidante during my awkward teen years; we often took long walks together when He listened to me explore possibilities for the future. He gave me the courage to leave home, strike out on my own, and become an independent adult. He led me to a mate and helped us raise our children. I'll admit I wasn't always as faithful to the relationship as He was, but even in those times I was aware of His "being there"—that I could call His name and He would respond.

Over and over as He verified His realness, an inner voice bubbled up within me, saying, "Yes, Brenda, there is a real Jesus." I could exclaim with the apostle John, "We have heard it [the word of life—Jesus], and we have seen it with our eyes; yes, we have seen it, and our hands have touched it. When this life became visible, we saw it; so we speak of it" (1 John 1:1–2 TEV).

I did not see Jesus in the flesh the way John did, but I saw Him operate in my life and in the lives of others. I heard His voice, I felt His touch. Like John, I had to say, "What we have seen and heard we announce to you also" (1 John 1:3 TEV).

I announce it to you, too, this Christmas. Yes! Jesus is real.

Chapter 3

OPEN *B*EFORE CHRISTMAS

Before Ben was born, when Jim and Joel were preschoolers, Bob and I moved away from family and friends in Indiana and Illinois so Bob could pursue graduate studies in Stillwater, Oklahoma. Our family of four settled into a tiny, 700-square-foot house just in time for the fall semester to begin.

We joined a church and began getting to know people. By Christmas, though, we had not made those vital connections that allow for warmth and closeness to occur naturally.

Bob was gone from home most of the time, spending hours studying in the library. So Jim, Joel, and I started to observe Christmas like we always did in traditional ways. We shopped for gifts, but that didn't take long because money was scarce. We baked Christmas cookies. We decorated a tree and put up other decorations around the house, but we missed having Bob around. We also missed having friends stop by to see our tree and sample our cookies.

We had the structure of Christmas—the decorations, a tree, the gifts, the food—but nothing to fill the structure to add warmth and richness. When I discussed my observation with Bob, I said, "It's like being all dressed up with nowhere to go."

I was still thinking about this when the mailman delivered a package marked "Open Before Christmas." With delight, Jim, Joel, and I quickly opened the gift. It was a punch-out cardboard nativity scene from an older friend back home. Perhaps she suspected that we might need something to do.

The boys and I immediately set to work popping out Mary, Joseph, baby Jesus, the shepherds, the wise men, the angel of the Lord, and the stable. While we assembled the pieces, I told the boys the story of Jesus' birth. Though I had read it to them before, I noticed an increased interest with this telling. The paper characters gave life to the story. When we finished, we arranged the pieces on the desk in the corner of our living room. I thought, "Well, that's the end of that. What a nice, brief activity!"

I was wrong. To my surprise, Jim and Joel often played with the figures. They acted out the story the way they played with trucks in the sand pile. Sometimes I stopped what I was doing to watch their reenactment of the drama. One day as I sat watching them, a memory of a Christmas Eve from my childhood surfaced.

Dormant No Longer

My mother (from whom I inherited my Martha tendencies) worked hard all day preparing a wonderful meal for Christmas Eve. One of my father's nephews was coming for dinner, and anticipation was in the air. We were going to have an enjoyable time together.

The meal, as with all of my mother's cooking, was delicious. When the dishes were washed and put away, Mother collapsed in the "big chair," the most comfortable chair in the living room. Dad, his nephew, my older sister, and my brother gathered around the dining table and began playing cards.

I bristled at this because our minister-grandfather frowned on playing cards. When he came to visit, we hid the cards, so I was certain that playing cards on Christmas Eve was a poor way to celebrate Jesus' birthday.

Okay, I'll admit that I might have been less indignant if I had been asked to play. The card players said my two younger sisters and I were too young. They didn't even want us hanging around the table where they were playing.

Banished to the living room, my sisters and I spent Christmas Eve pestering each other. We were restless and obnoxious. With nothing left on the Christmas agenda except opening gifts on Christmas morning, we couldn't find anything to do. Mother was quiet except for occasionally telling us to "Behave yourselves" and "Don't be so noisy." Her face looked sad and tired. After her hard day's work,

I certainly thought she deserved more than three restless girls at her feet. As the laughter and animated conversation from the card players drifted into the living room, I thought, *There has to be a better way to celebrate Jesus' birthday than this!*

Certainly that type of Christmas was not the norm at our house, and I realize that my memory of that evening may have been skewed. Mother may have been glad to rest in the "big chair" after her hard day's work! But I wasn't gladdened by the events of the evening. Instead I was distressed as only a self-righteous nine-year-old girl can be. Right then I determined that *someday* when I had a home of my own, when I had children, we would have a Christmas that really celebrated Jesus, one that really honored Him on his birthday. I didn't know how I would do it, but I knew I would.

As I watched Jim and Joel play, I wondered, *What happened to that determination?* My Christmases weren't any different than anyone else's. We hadn't ignored the meaning of the holiday in our Christmas celebrations, but neither had we made a deliberate effort to focus on Jesus' birth and its significance. As Jim broke my reverie with a question, I admitted I still wanted a Christ-centered Christmas, but I also had to admit I didn't know how and yet *someday* had arrived.

The Intentional Focus

Jim's question was one of several he and Joel asked me. Each conversation gave me an opportunity to link Christmas with Jesus. Of course, when I made the link for them, I made it for me, too. The wheels of my mind started turning. *Perhaps if I found ways to relate Jesus to my children, then I would have a Christmas that really celebrated Jesus.*

From then on, I began looking for ways to intentionally focus on Jesus at Christmas and what His coming to earth meant. *We were dressed up and we had somewhere to go!*

I felt good about my efforts, as if some missing piece of an inner puzzle had finally slipped into place. The uneasiness that haunted me disappeared. I didn't realize it then, couldn't even see it, but a "turning" was taking place. A choice was being made that would make "Mary" Christmases possible.

Chapter 4

TOO CUMBERED TO SEE

When it comes to Christmas many women feel they don't have a choice whether to be a Martha or a Mary. The busyness, the many expectations, they sheer weight of the joy of Christmas turns us into Marthas, bustling around making sure Christmas happens for our families, friends, and churches.

But f course, women do have choices. We're always deciding things—what to wear, where to go, what to make for dinner, what not to eat, what job to take, when to quit a job, on and on it goes. Any woman worth her salt will insist that women have choices, and yet there may remain areas of our lives where we don't see ourselves as having choices. It's almost as if we have blind spots—compartments of our lives where we can't see alternatives. Christmas is one of those compartments.

The Christmas Script

Long ago a script was written for women to follow, and it has been enlarged and magnified ever since until we are expected to be the Christmas magicians. As Jo Robinson and Jean Staeheli wrote in *Unplug the Christmas Machine*, women are: "responsible for transforming their families' everyday lives into a beautiful festival. No matter how busy they are, they bear the burden of pulling a magical celebration out of the hat year after year. Like their mothers before them, they are the planners, the shoppers, the decorators, the gift-wrappers, the bakers, the hostesses, and the house cleaners."

This script may have developed because many of the things associated with Christmas are things women usually do. Women buy and send more greeting cards than men. Women are the primary buyers of gifts and wrapping paper. Although many men cook, food preparation is more often associated with women. Women are usually more concerned about relationships than men.

The script is full of cultural expectations. These expectations are strong, and they wrap themselves tightly around women, pressuring us in such a way that we do not *feel* as if we have any choice about doing Christmas. That's what I meant when earlier I said women do not have a choice.

Martha, too, may have been bound by cultural expectations. Entertaining, being a hostess, and taking care of others was "woman's work" in her culture. Even though she could be decisive—she clearly chose to have Jesus in her home—she didn't see herself as having a choice once He arrived. When He crossed the threshold, she put on her "company glasses" and activated her people-pleaser gene. Responding to a script she didn't write, she couldn't see any alternatives. And yet Jesus' words to her when she complained about all she had to do implied that she did.

Martha's Choice

Frustrated, Martha said, "Lord, don't you care that my sister has left me to do the work by myself? Tell her to help me!" (Luke 10:40 NIV).

Jesus responded, "Martha, Martha, you are worried and upset about many things, but one thing is necessary. Mary has made the right choice, and it will not be taken away from her'" (Luke 10:41–42 HCSB).

I'm so glad that Jesus said Martha's name twice. This makes me certain His words were tinged with affection. There's always affection in my voice when I say my children's names twice when admonishing them. "Jim, Jim, put that knife down before you hurt yourself." "Joel, Joel, didn't I tell you to check both ways before crossing the street?" "Ben, Ben, how many times do I have to tell you not to run the riding lawn mower so fast?"

I imagine Jesus was shaking His head in exasperation and smiling at the same time when He talked to Martha. He saw all Martha was trying to do to please Him and to make Him comfortable. He saw that her intentions were good but still she needed some attitude adjustment.

Jesus didn't come out and say that Martha had a choice, but He said Mary did, and Mary was a product of the same culture. As a woman, Mary also would have been expected to do the entertaining and the cooking, but she saw herself as having options. She saw that she didn't have to always do as society dictated. She chose to sit at Jesus' feet.

Why didn't Martha make that same choice? She was a smart woman, so why didn't she welcome Jesus, offer Him a cup of water, and sit down beside Mary and listen to Him?

Too Cumbered to See

Different Bible versions describe Martha's frustration in various ways:

"Martha was distracted with all her preparations" (NASB).

"Martha was getting worried about having to wait on them so much" (Williams).

"Martha was upset over all the work she had to do" (GNT).

I like the King James Version's description best. It says Martha was "cumbered about much serving" (Luke 10:40 KJV). Being "cumbered" implies tightness, suggesting that Martha felt bound by the stress she was experiencing—not that she didn't want to have company! Jesus was a celebrity and a friend; it was a special honor to have Him in her home and she wanted things to go well. Once inside the door, though, as noted earlier, her responsibilities snowballed. And Martha, being the good woman that she was, was determined to handle them all. With her eyes straight ahead, she focused on entertaining the way she always had. If someone had said to her, "Slow down, Martha, relax and don't try so hard," it would have been asking the impossible. She might as well have been wearing blinders because she couldn't see any other way to entertain Jesus.

Being encumbered interferes with seeing alternatives; it clouds our vision. I know because I've experienced this effect of stress many times. Just last December, for example, I was supposed to teach the international mission study at our church. As the time drew near, I couldn't see how I could prepare for it, complete other projects I was committed to, plus get ready for Christmas and handle some family concerns. I didn't want to disappoint the missions council or renege on my responsibility, and yet I couldn't do it all. I stewed about this dilemma; I even woke up in the middle of the night thinking about it. Finally I confessed my dilemma to the council. I said, "Can you help me think of some alternatives?"

They threw out various possibilities. One said, "Why don't you ask Kim to teach the study?"

"Perfect," I said. The next day I contacted Kim, and she agreed to do it.

Kim, a member of our church, was very knowledgeable in missions and a capable person; she had helped me with projects before. Why hadn't I thought of Kim when I was stewing over my dilemma? My vision was clouded because I was encumbered by stress. The minute her name was mentioned my vision improved.

What's interesting about this is that my vision improved in other areas too. I not only saw a solution to the missions study dilemma, but my other projects and holiday preparation didn't appear as intimidating. My family concerns seemed more manageable, and even my worship was brighter. Although my Sunday morning worship was not directly related to any of my challenges, it too was affected by my being encumbered. I couldn't focus clearly because I kept thinking about all I had to do. Stress affects our ability to worship; stress affects our ability to see Jesus.

To see Jesus, to sit at his feet, to hear Him speak, and to experience His presence—what we are seeking in a Mary Christmas—is a spiritual encounter. It will be real but it won't be the same as Martha's, who had Jesus in the flesh as a guest in her home. It won't be the same as Mary's, who could hear His audible voice and touch His body. If we want to see Jesus, we need spiritual eyes to see. We need unencumbered eyes.

Chapter 5

ALL I *W*ANT FOR CHRISTMAS...

A question that is commonly asked around this time of year is: "What do you want for Christmas?"

We ask others what they want so we'll buy presents that will make them happy and please them. We ask little children what they want so we can see their eyes light up with anticipation. Then we plot and to plan how we can make their dreams come true. My mother encouraged us to write our names beside things we wanted in the Christmas catalogs. I did the same with my children. Jim, Joel, and Ben spent hours poring over the catalogs, thinking and writing their names in pencil in case they changed their minds. They weren't free to write their names by everything they wanted because their Santa had a price limit! So they had to think about what they *really wanted*.

We don't usually ask ourselves "What do I want for Christmas?" although more and more advertisers are encouraging us to. "Want to make sure you get what *you* want this Christmas? Buy your own gift. Go ahead and splurge on yourself. You deserve it." Dwelling too long on what you want can encourage dissatisfaction and discontentment, yet I've discovered that when it comes to having a "Mary" Christmas, it is an important question to ask.

Heightens the Sense of Possibility

As my sons pored over Christmas catalogs, considering their options, they dreamed of Christmas, and they imagined various scenarios that could take place. Jim looked at the football uniforms and electronic football games and dreamed of the day he would be a football player. Joel paused often at the musical instrument section. He thought a guitar would be nice. He could see himself opening a huge package on Christmas morning and strumming a guitar in the days afterwards. When Ben looked at the electric trains and saw the layouts in the catalog, he imagined putting the track together and the fun he would have engineering the train. The boys talked about what they wanted with each other and sometimes with Bob and me. Knowing Santa's budget the way I did, I marveled at their hopefulness and sense of expectancy. Anything was possible.

I long ago quit looking at Christmas catalogs the way Jim, Joel, and Ben did, but I do pore over December magazines for women. If I can manage it, I like to put aside the holiday issues when they arrive in mid-

November. Then on Thanksgiving night, when the "big meal" is over, the guests have gone, the dishes are washed and put away, and family members are each quietly doing their own thing after the hubbub of the day, I like to nestle in a comfy chair and look at the magazines.

If anyone asked me what I was doing, I wouldn't say "dreaming." I'd say, "I'm looking for ideas," or "A new recipe would be nice; I'm tired of fixing the same things." And yet I am dreaming. I look at the pictures of decorated houses, inside and out. I see the way mantles and trees are decorated. I note the recipes and craft ideas, even though I don't do crafts. I read the gift suggestions and like Jim, Joel, and Ben, I think about "what I want for Christmas."

As a Martha, I'm not thinking about sweaters, perfume, jewels, or bathrobes for myself, although there's nothing wrong with that. I'm thinking about our home, how I can create an ambiance for celebration, how I can make food that family members and guests will like, and how I can set a lovely table. The same sense that anything is possible grows inside me as I scan the pages. "Umm, that would be nice." "I like that." "That's a good idea." I clip out recipes. I fold the page corners over in the magazines that have ideas I may want to go back to if I have time.

Truthfully, most of the ideas I will never use. It is the process of looking and thinking that I enjoy. It gets me in a holiday mood and inspires me. It loosens the cords of expectations so they don't feel as tight. That Thanksgiving evening, I feel as if I have some control over the quality of our Christmas. I am a woman with alternatives; I am a woman who has choices.

Do you see how thinking about what we want heightens the sense of possibility and helps us see alternatives? It doesn't mean we are selfish, but it does improve our vision. It weakens the stronghold of those cords of expectations and means we aren't tied to a script someone else has written. It means we have choices.

Knowing What You Want

Perhaps this book can be a catalog or magazine for you. As you flip through the pages and read the reflections, I'm not expecting you to duplicate what I do, to have Christmases just like mine. Rather, I want to encourage you to dream a little and think about the kind of Christmas you want. Even writing out a list of what you want and mulling over it may raise your sense of possibility and enable you to see alternatives. Or talking to others might give you ideas. We can be women who see alternatives and make choices. Choice is important if we want a Mary Christmas. Martha was so encumbered that she didn't even see she had a choice. Mary saw that she did have options, and she made the "right choice."

I don't know if I would have ever started seeing myself as having Christmas alternatives if it were not for the surfacing of that dormant dream of having a Christmas that focused on Jesus. That's when I knew what I wanted. At the time I began a turning process—even though it wasn't a conscious choice, a choice was still being made—that would turn my eyes toward Jesus; I began to continually turn toward Him. In that turning, I discovered that a Mary Christmas is possible.

Making a choice can be a conscious, major event marked by a drum roll or signing on a dotted line somewhere. But it doesn't have to be. Choice can be a graduate turning, or a mental assent, such as it was for me, when you know what you want for Christmas.

Chapter 6

Do You Hear What Martha Hears?

Have you noticed how choosing seems easy when it is someone else's decision? As you hear a friend describe her situation, see her perplexed look, and observe her wringing her hands, you know what she should do. Her alternatives and the best choice are so clear that you wonder, *Why doesn't she see what to do and just do it?*

It is easy to regard Martha in the same way. We can easily see the choice she should have made. Any person knows that relationships should have priority over work and entertaining. We should never get so busy that we miss what is truly important. The right choice is so obvious that we may be tempted to think, *If I were Martha I would have forgotten about the meal and sat beside Mary.*

Maybe the reason we have such pristine vision about the choices of others is because we don't hear what they hear. A woman's befuddlement or indecisiveness is never just about what she sees, it is also about what she hears.

What Martha Heard

Martha was encumbered because of what she heard. I don't mean noisy surroundings or the sounds of people socializing. What I am suggesting is that she may have heard the voices of cultural expectations—those voices that say, "You should be a good cook," and "You ought to have a clean house," and "If you were really a capable homemaker, you would have everything organized." Inner voices may have kept Martha busy, scurrying around anxiously, trying to please. And if she had chosen to sit at Jesus' feet, they may have still nagged at her. "You ought to get Jesus a glass of water." "Have the disciples been fed? You should check on them."

Do you hear what Martha hears? Yes, in a way we all do. We all hear inner voices at some time or other (and we're not talking schizophrenia or paranoia here!) that influence our choices and our behavior. However, we don't all seem to be influenced by them in the same way. Mary, exposed to the same cultural expectations, must not have been affected in the same way as Martha. While I don't know this for sure, I think those of us with the people-pleaser gene and the must-do-it-right gene are pressured more by inner voices than others, especially during December. We hear voices telling us how Christmas ought to be done and nagging us about what we should be doing. Not all women are going to hear the same voices—they can be voices from our past, our present, the future, and even from all three!

The Voices of Christmas Past

One inner voice a woman may hear is that of her mother, telling her what to do. Our mothers' teaching and guidance about being a homemaker and about being a hostess are still very much with most of us. If your mother was a particularly dominant person—and children often see their mother that way, even when she wasn't—her voice is incessant and compelling and you can't bring yourself to disobey. Somewhere on the way to growing up, a mother's guidance turned into laws that can't be broken!

But even if a woman's mother was not domineering, but was especially adept at creating Christmases full of good memories, she speaks through your must-do-it-right gene. The voice urges you to replicate the Christmases of your childhood. You launch into doing Christmas just the way your mother did, never stopping to consider that her life and responsibilities may have been very different from yours. As a child, you might never have noticed all the work behind the scenes that your mother did to make those kinds of Christmases possible. It seemed so easy for her, but now as you try to recreate those Christmases, you're exhausted and you wonder, "How did Mom ever do it?"

On the other hand, some women may not want to repeat their childhood Christmases. Their inner voice is repeatedly saying, "Don't let Christmas for your children be like the Christmases you had." Maybe they were sad or barren or full of discord. In response, these women determine everything will go smoothly in their family's Christmas. They will have warm, harmonious get-togethers, and the voice never suggests that the women might not have control of all the variables. The voice implies they can do it no matter what.

Or maybe a voice from a past Christmas that speaks to you is something someone said that stuck in your memory. Your child cried in disappointment over her gifts and said, "Mom, didn't Santa Claus come this year?" Your teenager quickly left the room after opening gifts. You heard him mumble under his breath, "Why didn't I get the jacket I wanted? I showed it to her when we were at the mall." You spent a lot of money on a gift for a friend. It was a silk scarf in colors that would enhance her eyes and hair. When she opened it, she looked at it and said, "Oh, that's nice," set it aside, and changed the subject. Ever since, the words have haunted you, so you work yourself into frenzy every Christmas trying to get everyone on your list exactly what they want.

The Voices of Christmas Present

December is the season of domesticity, when hearts and minds turn toward hearth and home. We want cozy Christmases with good food—all homemade, of course. We want a picture-perfect holiday. Those December magazines that inspire me may have the opposite effect on some women. As they look at the pictures, the voices in their heads say, "The message is clear: if you can't cook Christmas Eve dinner, Christmas breakfast, *and* Christmas dinner, plus clean the house, and make sure the kids home from college have clean sheets, and be cheerful while you work, you are a weakling."

In this season of domesticity, a woman may suddenly evaluate her role as a mother. The voice of guilt speaks up and reminds her of what she didn't do the rest of the year. She suddenly is motivated to make up to her children for all the songs not sung, books not read, outings not taken, and construction paper not glued while she was holding down a job or being terribly busy with projects.

Surrounded by the excess and abundance, she feels guilty about the poor. She can't really enjoy the holiday unless she does something for all the unfortunates in her area. It is as if they suddenly come into view even though they were also poor in January, February, and June, when the inner voice of guilt was silent. Now it says she must do something.

Even walking by Christmas decorations in a discount store or department store can trigger voices. You look at the decorated trees and the displays, and a voice starts saying, "You ought to get new decorations. What you have looks so dismal." You may have been perfectly happy with your droopy little Christmas tree. You thought it was cute and had character, and then you go to a friend's house where the tree is sophisticated and stately. A voice says, "You should have a tree like that. Your little tree is pathetic."

The Voices of Christmases Yet to Come

A woman may not only want happiness for the moment, but she may want her Christmas celebrations to be so good that her friends will rave for months or her children will have wonderful memories to recall. In your mind's eye, you see them in the future as young adults. They are attending a party where they are asked, "What traditions did you have at your home? What was your favorite memory of Christmas? What was the best gift you ever received?" You shudder to think that if you don't do things right, they might not have any good answers.

This past Christmas as I was buying greeting cards, I opened one that said, "Have the kind of Christmas that in the years to come you can recount good memories." I thought, *What kind of Christmas wish is that?* It sounded like more pressure on the Christmas Magician. Not only must she pull the whole show together, but she is also made to feel responsible for making it so spectacular that her children or her guests can recall it for years to come. I hope the recipient of the card has better luck than I did. A number of things that I initiated in our family's celebrations we repeated for years, but when one of my sons was in college, he was asked at a party what Christmas traditions we had. He answered, "None. The only tradition we had was that we celebrated." Well, at least I got one thing right!

Fortunately, I never experienced an inner voice that said, "Create memorable traditions for your children." But I did hear other voices. We all have to learn to challenge and deal with these voices if we are to have a Mary Christmas.

I'd like to think making choices isn't necessary to having a Mary Christmas. I wish heaven would just open and bless me with a heavenly host singing and inviting me to meet Jesus at a stable somewhere. Or send me a star that would show me the way to Jesus. I would rather heaven take the initiative. But Christmas is, and always has been, about making choices. Mary made the right choice. If I want to see Jesus, hear Him speak, and experience His presence, then I need to stop listening to the voices of Christmas past, present, and yet to come. I need to find out how to listen to Jesus. What kind of hearing is involved?

The Bible tells us that Jesus often said: "He who hath ears to hear, let him hear." I want to have ears to hear Jesus.

Chapter 7

No Goodyear Blimp *H*overed Overhead

Sometimes, when looking back, I think the whole world must have been aware of the significance of Jesus' birth. Everyone knew that the child born in a stable was the Son of God, the promised Messiah, but there was no Goodyear blimp hovering overhead, so the event wasn't televised. Neither were camera crews running around on the ground trying to get great pictures to broadcast on the evening news. Reporters weren't there to write down every word that Mary and Joseph said or to record Jesus' first cry. Commentators weren't interpreting the news, telling listeners that this event was of monumental importance.

Even many of the locals didn't pick up on the significance. To the residents at the inn where Joseph and Mary were turned away, to the visitors in Bethlehem for the Roman census, to the residents of Bethlehem, Jesus was just another Jewish baby being born to a poor, peasant couple. They had no idea that the eternal God was entering time, that the Son of God was being born of a woman, and that the event would divide all human history.

There were a few, though, who did acknowledge that something special was happening. They were the shepherds, the wise men, and Simeon and Anna. Each was spiritually ready to receive because they had ears to hear.

Ears to Hear

Every speaker and teacher knows about ears to hear, and it has nothing to do with volume as in "testing one, two, three." Rather, someone with ears to hear has a receptive spirit that takes in what the speaker says, connects with it, grasps its meaning, and frequently responds. A speaker can give the same presentation to two different groups and one group will respond with, "That's the best speech I ever heard. Your insights were so helpful," and the other group mumbles, "Thanks for coming today." In the classroom, a student with ears to hear may ask questions and take notes, and even his eyes might light up, while across the aisle another student—without ears to hear—doodles and glances out the window.

When Jesus spoke, He often told interesting, thought-provoking stories, and made unusual statements—the kinds of things that make a person want to listen. Yet Jesus knew there were people in the audience who would not pick up on the meaning of the stories and discern their applicability. He also realized there were people in the audience for other reasons, and no matter how well He told a story, they would not discern the meaning. Some were there out of curiosity, some to get what they could from Him, some to ridicule Him, and some to just be a part of the action. They were not spiritually sensitive people.

Having "ears to hear" means more than hearing with our ears, although obviously this is a part of it. It may also involve our eyesight, because that is another way we "take in" things, but having "ears to hear" is being spiritually aware and receptive. It is responding as the shepherds, the wise men, Simeon, and Anna did. They weren't randomly selected people. They were the ones who recognized Jesus for who He was when He was born because they had ears to hear.

The Shepherds

The night Jesus was born in Bethlehem, some shepherds in the nearby countryside were spending the night with their sheep. "An angel of the Lord appeared to them, and the glory of the Lord shone over them" (Luke 2:9a). The angel announced Jesus' birth, "This very day in David's town your Savior was born—Christ the Lord!" (Luke 2:11). Suddenly a great host of heavenly beings appeared beside the angel, singing praises to God.

Not everyone who sees unusual beings in the sky would say they came from God. They could be creatures from space! The angel of the Lord did say to them, "Don't be afraid!" (Luke 2:10b). And what does the "glory of the Lord" look like? How would you recognize it? The shepherds saw the glory, and they recognized the angelic chorus as coming from God. They responded by rushing to Bethlehem to see Jesus.

I think that the nature of their work had prepared them for this moment. The shepherds were alone most of the time. Being away from the distractions of community living and activities, they probably reflected upon life. In reflecting, they turned to God and became spiritually sensitive to the way He works. Because they had made the most of their solitude, they recognized God at work and could see His glory all around when the angel of the Lord and the heavenly host visited them.

The Wise Men

Some time after Jesus' birth, some men who studied the stars came from the East looking for a king (Matthew 2:1–12). We do not know the names of these men, nor do we know exactly where they came from. We do know that they were dedicated to a search for truth and they carefully examined evidence that came to their attention. As they scanned books and sky and land, they saw an unusual star that intrigued them. From their studies, they knew an unusual star could mean a king was born. They had to learn more! Eagerly, they pursued truth. They were the sort of people who were willing to go to great lengths to try to understand why certain things happened. At great effort, they investigated and found the Son of God. By the discipline of their searching, they were able to perceive what others didn't see. Their earnest curiosity cultivated their spiritual sensitivity.

Simeon and Anna

When Joseph and Mary took baby Jesus to the temple in Jerusalem, two elderly saints, Simeon and Anna, recognized Him. They had spent most of their days in the house of the Lord, waiting confidently to see the unfolding of God's purpose. Shaped by a lifetime of worship, they came to know God so well that they could recognize Him in a baby. The Jews were not expecting the Messiah to come as a baby. They were expecting an adult, a powerful military deliverer. When Jesus came as a baby, Simeon and Anna recognized Him as the deliverer of God's salvation for His people. They knew who Jesus was because they had so identified their affections with God that they were able to recognize what others didn't.

Other than the shepherds, the wise men, Simeon, and Anna, no one else, except Mary and Joseph of course, had any idea of the significance of Jesus' birth. Many eyes looked on baby Jesus as people view new babies, but only the eyes that had been spiritually sharpened discerned who He really was. Many ears heard His cries, heard His parents speak, heard the reports of the shepherds, heard the inquiries of the wise men, and heard the testimonies of Simeon and Anna, but only those who were spiritually ready heard God.

If we want "ears to hear," then we may need to cultivate our spiritual awareness and receptivity.

Here's where the Marys of this world may have an advantage over the Marthas.

Spiritual Cultivation

Just as Martha has gained a reputation for busyness, her sister Mary has gained one for being sensitive. She picked up on information around her that others missed. She sensed Jesus' feelings and how to please Him. She had the foresight to recognize impending developments before they fully materialized and became obvious to others. With such keen sensitivity, she naturally gravitated toward sitting at His feet and listening to Him. Making the right choice wasn't as complicated for her as it was for Martha.

I believe Martha was sensitive at one time, too, because we all start out that way. God created us to be spiritual creatures as well as emotional, physical, and mental. So right from the first, we have a desire toward the spiritual, an impulse to connect with God and a desire to interact with Him.

The sensitivity we are born with can be diminished or enhanced by many things, such as the way we were raised, the responsibilities we have, or the way others respond to us. Since Martha was the responsible one, the homeowner, the one who looked after details, she didn't have time to cultivate this part of her nature.

The kinds of things I've been writing about in this book can affect our spiritual sensitivity. Expectations that wrap themselves around us, the many things we see that need to be done, and the "you shoulds" and the "you oughts" we hear can erode our spiritual sensitivity. It's this side of us that we want to reclaim and cultivate if we want to see Jesus and to hear Him speak. This doesn't mean we have to change our personality and turn into a Mary. It means being spiritually ready to recognize His appearance and to appreciate His presence. The examples of the shepherds, the wise men, Simeon and Anna—about whom I'm going to write more in the pages ahead—and others will help us find moments when we can feel the essence of Christmas and know that Jesus is present. I call these moments my "midnight clear moments."

Spiritual Clarity

I first gave Jesus' appearances this label because they often came during late-night hours when the rest of the household was asleep, and I was still up wrapping presents, planning my guest list, or addressing invitations. The label stuck, though, because of the spiritual clarity involved. I knew Jesus was visiting me and I was learning from Him about His nature, His personality, or His mission.

Those moments didn't always come on Christmas Eve or Christmas Day, but they came during the season with such clarity that for a brief time, I was no longer Martha scurrying about frantic with worry. I was sitting at Jesus' feet, learning from Him, feeling His presence, listening to Him speak, and interacting with Him. I was having a Mary Christmas.

Chapter 8

SILENT NIGHTS MAKE FOR *H*OLY NIGHTS

E. B. White once said, "To perceive Christmas through its wrapping becomes more difficult with every year." I would say, "To perceive Christ in Christmas through its wrapping becomes more difficult with every year."

White said we need some kind of ear trumpet like hunters use to hear the distant sounds of the hounds. We need some kind of long, wide-on-one-end instrument that would penetrate the wrapping and connect us with meaning.

What kind of ear trumpet would we need to hear Jesus? From the shepherds, we learn that solitude can improve our hearing. Quiet moments help us to have a Mary Christmas.

Silent Nights and Quiet Days

The angels appeared to shepherds—a group on the

hillside—when they gave them the news of Jesus' birth, but most of the time shepherds worked alone. They had the company of the sheep and probably a dog, but rarely other humans to distract them from their thoughts or engage them in intense conversations. They lived very quiet lives. They were out near the simplicities of existence and away from the distractions of artificial sophistication, so conditions were optimum for concentration.

In this unencumbered, simple existence, they could develop their reflective powers. As they leaned on their staffs, they could think about life and wonder about God. Through careful consideration and contemplative thought, we naturally draw close to God. When we are still, and listen, we can recognize God at work.

The shepherds' work was in the outdoors. I think outdoor work helps people develop their reflective ability. The natural surroundings, the clouds, the stars at night must have been awe-inspiring, calling their attention to the Designer behind it all, especially at night when the sheep were bedded down. As they kept a watchful eye out for predators and robbers, they must have gazed at the night sky and were filled with wonder.

The nature of the shepherds' work enabled them to develop their spiritual perception and receptivity. That's why their silent night became a holy night when the angels came and delivered God's message to them. Solitude reduces distractions, facilitates thinking, and improves our listening ability, sometimes giving a pristine quality to what we experience; this is exactly what Bernie May, former director of Wycliffe Bible Translators, discovered.

A Pure and Clear Revelation

When Bernie was a missionary pilot, flying Bible translators for the Jungle Aviation and Radio Service in Peru, he and his wife Nancy were nostalgic for Christmas back home in Pennsylvania. It was their third Christmas away from home, but their three boys were excited as Christmas approached. To the boys, Peru was home. And the air around the mission center, with more than 300 translators and support personnel, was festive.

The week before Christmas, Bernie's flight coordinator asked him to make an emergency flight to the Maranon River basin, carrying medical supplies to an Indian tribe where there had been an epidemic. He scheduled Bernie to return to Nancy and the boys on the evening of December 23.

Bernie made the five-hour flight without incident. The old Aeronca plane with its bulky pontoons droned through the scattered clouds and safely landed on the river near the Indian village. He planned to spend the night at the village, sleeping in a jungle lean-to between two palm trees, and depart the next morning for home.

During the night, however, he heard rain splattering on the thatch roof over his head. When he awoke in the morning the entire river basin was covered with fog and rain. There would be no flying that day.

It rained all day and through the next night. Christmas Eve was the same. The clouds were down to the tops of the trees. The rain fell steadily.

Bernie slipped on a poncho and trudged through the village down to the river's edge. The plane was tied against the bank, rocking gently on the rain-splattered water. He crawled out on a pontoon and sat under the wing, feeling desperately sorry for himself.

It was Christmas Eve, and night was descending on the jungle. He knew there was no way he could get back home.

Back in Pennsylvania, his folks would have returned from church and his mother would be getting the turkey ready. Outside, the snow would be falling. The big tree, with the star on top, would be standing as always in its corner.

Back at the mission center, six hours away, Nancy and the boys would be sitting at home alone. They knew that he was stuck in the jungle because he had been able to radio them. He would not be with family for Christmas.

"Oh, God," he moaned, "I'm in the wrong place."

More than anything else he wanted to be home for Christmas.

Instead, he sloshed his way back to his hut in the little village. He shared some yucca with a couple of Indian children, and read them the Christmas story out of the Bible, doing his best to translate it so they could understand.

That night, under his mosquito net, Bernie had a visitation from God—a midnight clear moment like the shepherds experienced on the hills outside of Bethlehem. There were no angels, and no bright light, but the clarity was there, and so was a voice. As he lay in his hammock, desperately homesick, he heard God say: "My son, this is what Christmas is all about. Jesus left heaven and on Christmas morning He woke up in the 'wrong place'—a stable in Bethlehem. Christmas means leaving home, not going home. My only begotten Son did not come home for Christmas—He left His home to be with you."

Bernie opened his eyes. Overhead, through the mosquito net, he could see the brown palm-thatch leaves that formed the ceiling of the lean-to. Beneath him was the hard-packed dirt floor. All around was the sound of gently falling rain.

But out there in the darkness were men and women, boys and girls, tiny babies—all part of the Indian tribe. He was there, away from home Christmas Eve, because Jesus left His home on Christmas. Bernie was there because Jesus said, "As the Father hath sent Me, even so send I you."

During the night the rain stopped. On Christmas Day Bernie was able to take off from the river and by nightfall he was back with his loved ones. He went back knowing in an indelible way that Christmas is God's ultimate missionary outreach. In the wrong place for Christmas, a silent night turned into a holy night.

Being alone would probably feel wrong to us too. Christmas is for celebrating with others, having company, visiting, gathering together. Being alone is something most try to avoid at Christmas, but

Bernie's story and the experience of the shepherds remind us that solitude creates an environment for spiritual encounters. If I want holy moments, I may need to look for times when I can turn my thoughts and attention toward God.

Finding the Right Time

My favorite time for solitude has been—and is—early morning before the rest of the household is awake, although one of my friends says that he's not sure God is awake at 5:00 in the morning! I assure him that He is, and tell him I prefer to meet Him then because the day is fresh and so am I. Once the Christmas tree is up, though, I also like reflecting at the end of the day. In a quiet house, after the other family members have gone to bed, I like to meditate by the lighted tree. This only works if you have don't have blinking lights! Flashing lights, in my opinion, are part of the Christmas wrapping that interferes with meditation!

Even times when we are not completely alone can have the "feel" of solitude. As our sons matured into young men, a lot of our Christmas noise—the good sounds of boisterous laughter and play—diminished as they carved out lives for themselves. I remember the first Christmas it was just three of us. Ben was in Africa and Joel was in Japan, so Bob and I went to see Jim in Chicago. That must have been one of Chicago's coldest Christmases. The wind blew off of Lake Michigan and chilled us to the bone, while our boots crunched several layers of snow on the ground.

Jim, Bob, and I are all good talkers, but by Christmas Eve we had covered all the updates of family and friends and current events. Our conversation died down, so when we went to the Christmas Eve service in a large downtown church we silently waited for the service to begin. It wasn't quite solitude and yet it was. People around us talked, but I didn't communicate with them, nor they with me. Everyone was into his own group of family and friends. I felt alone.

In my quiet spot, I watched the people. Some were dressed in fine fur coats and expensive clothing. Then there were those, like us, dressed in our J.C. Penney finest. Homeless people were there too. You wondered if they were there for the service or the warmth, and I wouldn't have faulted them at all if it were just for warmth. I noticed different races—blacks, whites, Hispanics, and Asians—and different ages. Old people were there, but so were college students and children. I thought, *What a cross section of society is here tonight!*

A soloist stood among the red poinsettias that flanked the altar and sang "O Holy Night." That's when the tears began falling and I knew the Spirit of Jesus was touching me. *Oh, it was indeed a holy night when He was born. It was like no other night because the Son of God was bringing His love and forgiveness to men and women and boys and girls of all races and economic levels.* Of course, I already knew that in an academic way, but in my silent night I had a new appreciation for the Holy Night as the wonder of God's love bubbled up inside me. In my "felt" solitude, I found a right time for experiencing Jesus.

Chapter 9

HAVE YOURSELF A *M*ARY LITTLE CHRISTMAS

Miss Manners says, "If the holiday gerunds—decorating, cooking, shopping, stuffing—seem daunting, it is probably because you have neglected to do the first one, and have skipped to doing the last. The last is grousing. The first is pruning." She insists that pruning is necessary to retaining good cheer. I see it as necessary to a Mary Christmas because God speaks to us in simplicity.

Uncluttered Living

I am not saying that God speaks only to people living simple lives; God speaks in many ways to people in various circumstances. What I have noticed, though, is that we are more likely to have "ears to hear" when our lives aren't cluttered with possessions, obligations, and activities. Living simply nurtures spiritual perception and receptivity.

The shepherds lived simply in addition to living quiet lives. Even though they had concerns about the sheep under their care, worry about possessions didn't mar their reflection. A shepherd had a mantle, made probably of sheepskin with the fleece on, which he turned inside out in cold weather. He had a scrip or wallet containing a small amount of food. He had a sling for a weapon and a staff with a crook in it for managing the flock.

With few possessions, the shepherds weren't distracted by floors to sweep, vehicles to repair, cabinets to clean, collections to organize, and meetings to attend. They could be attentive to the sheep and develop their perceptive powers at the same time.

Christmas in our culture isn't conducive to developing spiritual perception. *Excess, elaborate,* and *expensive* are words that describe Christmas, not the word *simple.* Celebration, by nature, calls for some indulgence and I'm all for that, but it can sometimes take on a life of its own and grow!

Each year we add to our Christmas celebrations and make them bigger and better. We want our celebrations larger or more elaborate than we've had before. The number of decorations grows; we start Christmas collections that must be protected, stored, and dusted! The commercialization of Christmas tempts us to buy more and more. It makes us want things we don't need and makes us think they are absolute necessities. And the weight of most of this falls on—you guessed it!—

the Marthas of this world, and they begin to grumble. No wonder Miss Manners suggested pruning for good cheer.

Clipping Christmas

I remember being surprised when a friend told me about pruning her Christmas tree. As a woman who enjoys doing a little yard work, I was aware of the need to keep trees, shrubs, and rose bushes pruned, but I had never heard of anyone pruning a Christmas tree they bought. Carole mentioned taking the shears to a cut tree she had bought. She shaped it to her liking when she got the tree home from the garden center. Ever since, I've nipped mine and have enjoyed the results.

Simplifying our Christmas can also bring positive results when we prune and shape it so it will be more pleasurable and meaningful. Each woman who wants this kind of Christmas will have to decide for herself where and what she will prune. Here's one of those times when knowing what you want for Christmas comes in handy! You can leave untouched those things that are most important to you and snip away at those things that aren't. Here are some nips and tucks I've taken through the years to simplify our Christmas.

Shear by sharing. In various ways, I've asked my family members to share the workload. When our sons were in elementary school, I prepared a work chart where I listed various jobs to be done in December. I told them I would pay them for their work. Half of what they earned must go for a gift for Jesus. The other half they could keep for themselves, to do with what they wanted. Payment for the jobs came in multiples of dimes, so the amount could be easily divided. We counted out the dimes for Jesus, put them in an offering envelope designated for foreign missions, and placed it in the offering plate at church.

When the boys became teenagers, I began to think that scene of my mother being all worn out at Christmas Eve from fixing dinner alone—the scene I mentioned in chapter 3—was going to replay itself at our house. I didn't want to be left all alone in the kitchen fixing the Christmas meal while the others watched television in the living room. I wanted togetherness! On Thanksgiving, on the way to visit relatives for dinner, I had a captive audience in the car. I explained that I wanted us to work together to prepare the meal. They were agreeable, and we divided up the menu with each person preparing a separate dish and me fixing the meat.

My family readily responded to my request for help and would do so more often if I would let them help with the workload. When Bob sees me scurrying around, trying to get things done, he says, "I'll be glad to help. Just let me know what you want me to do." Can you believe that I often ignore his offer? It's because of that "must do it right" gene. I'm afraid he'll serve the fruit salad in a margarine tub or put the forks on the napkins instead of beside the napkins. When you share the load, you have to surrender your standards. You can't grab the margarine tub back or glare at the one he placed among your fine china. That will put an end to future cooperation. He who does the job gets to determine how it will be done.

Cut back on décor. One simplifier—one where I didn't have to surrender any standards—occurred to me the day I realized that what goes up must come down. As my Christmases were growing and the work list was correspondingly increasing, I realized how much work Martha had to do *after* Christmas as well as before Christmas. All the decorations had to be taken down, packed away, and stored. So I started getting less out and I found that not all the decorations were necessary. I learned that enough was needed to indicate that something special was happening, to have a celebrative atmosphere and a warm ambiance. Beyond that, the rest of the decorations can be scaled back, eliminating a lot of work before and after Christmas.

Trim the gift list. I sighed with relief the day our extended family began reducing the number of people we bought gifts for. First we decided the adults (my siblings, their spouses, and me) would draw names and everyone buy for the children and our parents. Then another year the adults stopped giving any gifts to each other and focused on the children and my parents. Then the children started drawing names, and as they got older eventually quit exchanging gifts. Now we children buy for our parents, and my mother buys for all of us, including something for all her grandchildren. My mother delights in gift giving and she delightfully plans for it. Pruning for her would never include trimming her list. We will all prune in different ways in light of what is most important to us and in light of what will make our Christmas more pleasurable and meaningful.

Crop the ideal picture. In that mental dream picture of Christmas that we all carry around within us, the ideal of gift-giving is to really think about the person for whom you are buying a gift. We are sensitive to his or her likes and dislikes. We try to find out what he or she wants and give something that will really please him or her. This is the way we show we care. When you are buying gifts for many people and there's a time crunch, it is hard to exercise this ideal. That's why I gave my children Christmas catalogs to look at when they were young. It was simpler than trying to figure out what they wanted.

As the boys became older teens, they were beyond looking at the Christmas catalogs. That was kid stuff! I tried to keep up with their interests and sense what they really wanted, but this became increasingly difficult. They responded by developing lists and handing them to me. Searching for and buying what was on their list became a time-consuming *obligation* in which I began to question if it really was more blessed to give than to receive. That thought was a clue it was time for some simplifying.

I arranged a "date" with one son at a time and took him for a one-time shopping trip. I told him how much money I had to spend and let him decide how to spend it. We shopped together, did a lot of conversing while we looked, and he made the final selections. I took the gifts home and wrapped them, and when they opened the presents on Christmas Day, they said, "What a surprise! And it is just what I wanted!"

While it wasn't ideal, the joy of giving to my sons returned. I saved time by shopping once with each one, plus I enjoyed the one on-one time with each one. I began to view the shopping trip—not what we bought—as my gift to them. It wasn't an ideal gift, but still it was a gift, a gift that I was free to enjoy giving.

The Freedom of Simplicity

Like Miss Manner says, your good cheer returns when you prune your Christmas. Our pleasure will increase and so will our chances for having a Mary Christmas.

Simplifying Christmas frees us of some of the pressures of Christmas. It improves the quality of our Christmas. It brings joy and balance.

Simplicity also allows time for savoring and enjoyment instead of so much frantic rushing. It frees the senses to truly enjoy what we experience.

Simplifying Christmas frees up our mind so we can reflect on Jesus. We won't be distracted with so much clutter, details, and work! It will reduce the anxieties that encumber us. It frees up inner space so we have room in our hearts for Jesus.

Chapter 10

THE CHRISTMAS THAT CHANGED *A*LL CHRISTMASES

B y the time we were approaching our second
Christmas in Stillwater, our nation was being
affected by rapidly spiraling inflation. It became
increasingly difficult for me to stretch our small
salaries—Bob's as a graduate assistant and mine as a
writer—to cover our expenses. While Bob was
immersed in his studies, I contended with our income,
trying to make it stretch to meet our bills and put food
on the table. We never missed a meal, but I constantly
wondered how we would manage the next one.

The one luxury we wanted was a trip to see our
families over Christmas. My family lived in central
Illinois and Bob's mother lived in southeast Missouri.

In November Bob's mother gave us a check large
enough to cover the gas for the trip. Often I was
tempted to spend the money. Continually, it was a
debate between the trip or medicine, the trip or food,

etc. I was relieved when the time came for the trip so I wouldn't have to make any more decisions.

We left Stillwater with the anxiety of *what-will-we-do-if-something-unexpected-happens* weighing heavy on our shoulders. We stopped first to see our fiends Bob and Margie in Broken Arrow.

Christmas of Contrast

Since the last time we had visited Bob and Margie, they had moved. We followed the phone directions they gave us, and found their new house in a subdivision. We rang the doorbell, and when the door opened, it framed a sight that could have been a magazine cover. Margie was dressed in a long evening gown. Behind her was a roaring fireplace with handsome leather chairs on each side and a perfectly decorated Christmas tree in the corner.

We stood there staring and not moving until Margie reached out and pulled us in. We must have looked like ragamuffins in contrast to her beautiful dress. She quickly explained the evening dress. She and Bob were going to a Christmas party. She encouraged us to make ourselves at home, letting Jim and Joel play with her sons while they were gone.

"Sure, that will be fine," I stuttered.

While she and Bob were gone and the children played, I couldn't help but notice how rich everything was. The newness was in stark contrast to our modest, well-worn house back in Stillwater. Margie had made Christmas goodies and had presents wrapped under the tree. I found myself thinking, *There's so much of everything.*

The next morning we said goodbye to Bob and Margie and went on to central Illinois. It was dark when we arrived at the home of my parents. They had been watching for us. Dad had turned on his outside Christmas lights. Mother had the house decorated with candles, wreaths, and Christmas flowers. Bowls of candy and nuts were all around. Their Christmas tree had presents stacked under it. My parents were people of modest means, but as I looked around their house all I could think was, *So much, so much, there's so much of everything.*

My sister and her husband stopped by to see us. She's a beautician and he's a barber. They took one look at our long, unstyled hair and offered to shampoo and cut our hair. Our hair hadn't been cut since August, so it really felt good.

As she cut my hair, Linda said, "I want to give you a permanent while you're home."

"But Linda," I said, "there's no way that I can pay for it."

"Let it be my Christmas present to you," Linda said. "I hope you don't mind, but we bought some Christmas presents for Jim and Joel. We thought you might need a little help this year. No one else in the family will have to know. We wrapped the gifts and put them under the tree 'from Santa Claus.'"

Tears trickled down my cheeks.

"What's wrong?" Linda asked. "Have I said something to hurt your feelings?"

"Oh, no," I answered, but I could say no more. I hadn't realized how hard our life had been until I saw what we had been missing. I was not jealous, but I couldn't help noticing. It was like seeing an oasis in the middle of a desert. I was touched by Linda's generosity, but something else touched me, too.

All evening a phrase kept bobbing around in my head. I let it surface. *He became poor. He became poor.* I knew the phrase was from one of the apostle Paul's letters, but I couldn't quite remember where it was found. When I got back to my parents' home, I checked a concordance to find it in 2 Corinthians 8:9—"For ye know the grace of our Lord Jesus Christ, that, though he was rich, yet for your sakes he became poor, that ye through his poverty might be rich" (KJV).

I hadn't given that verse much thought before, but that night its truth sank in. As I thought about His birth and His life, I realized He really did become poor.

The Realization

Jesus was born to poor parents. We know this because of the two pigeons Mary presented at her purification ceremony when she, Joseph, and baby Jesus visited the Temple in Jerusalem. (This was the occasion when Simeon and Anna recognized Jesus as the Messiah.) When a woman had borne a child, she was unclean until she brought to the Temple a lamb for a burnt offering and a young pigeon for a sin offering. That was a somewhat expensive sacrifice, and so the law stipulated that if she could not afford the lamb she might bring another pigeon instead. The offering of the two pigeons instead of the lamb and the pigeon was called the *Offering of the Poor*. It was the offering of the poor that Mary sacrificed.

By choice Jesus lived an impoverished life as an adult. During His three years of ministry, Jesus did not have a thing that He could call His own. When He was tired, He borrowed a fishing boat to lie down and sleep in. When He was thirsty, He asked the woman at the well to give Him a drink of water. When He wanted to teach a lesson about the bounds of church and civil society, He said, "Bring me a coin." Jesus had to depend on others for the donkey on which He made His entry into Jerusalem. He had to borrow the upper room where He shared the Passover meal with the Twelve and use the private garden of a friend for prayer.

Although Jesus fed the multitudes by way of miracles, He never used His divine power to provide for His own physical needs. Even after Jesus fasted for forty days, Satan could not successfully tempt Jesus to turn stones into bread.

He had no place to lay His head. He remarked to a would-be disciple, "Foxes have holes, and birds of the air have nests; but the Son of man has nowhere to lay his head" (Luke 9:58).

Jesus willingly left the riches of heaven to become poor. Even though everything the Heavenly Father had was His, Jesus chose to live a simple life. I wondered, *Had His adjustment ever been difficult? Did He ever long for the riches that were rightfully His? Did He ever contemplate a different way?*

As I thought about this—considered Jesus' coming from His point of view—I connected with Him. I had a new point of identity with Jesus—one I would need that winter and one that would affect all my Christmases to come.

The Developing Kinship

The unexpected—what we had feared—happened on our trip. Bob got sick while we were visiting his mother. After paying for his medicine, we had to borrow money from her to make the trip back to Stillwater.

When we returned home, our finances did not improve until Bob finished graduate school, but I no longer felt alone. I felt a kinship with Jesus. He understood what I was experiencing, and that was a great comfort to me. Sometimes as I had the checkbook and the bills out on the table, I could feel His nearness as if He were standing right beside me. Jesus became indelibly printed on my soul.

His indelible imprint affected all my future Christmases. I wanted to refrain from overindulgence, as it didn't fit His character or lifestyle. He lived a simple life and taught us to live simply. My celebration needed to reflect that. A new word entered my celebration terminology. *Appropriately*. It seemed to me if I were truly going to honor Jesus, then my celebration needed to be appropriate. It needed to reflect Him, His nature, and His mission.

Chapter 11

HAPPY BIRTHDAY, *J*ESUS

My friend Jan has food allergies, including tomatoes and white flour. When I want to honor her, I don't fix her spaghetti and French bread. For Christmas I made her some cookies without flour. The ingredients were simple, so the gift didn't cost very much, but Jan was as ecstatic in her response as if I had given her a thousand dollars. The cookies were good—but not that good!

My dad is not a reader, so I never give him books for his birthday, even though I would like to because I think books make great gifts. (A writer would feel this way, wouldn't she?) I do give him word puzzle magazines because he likes to work puzzles.

My husband is not a coffee drinker. Even though I am and I think having a cup is a perfect way to end a meal, I don't plan on surprising him with cinnamon hazelnut coffee for his birthday because he would be more pleased with ribs and barbecue sauce.

When we truly want to honor another person, to make his or her birthday special, we think about him or her. What would he like? What would please her? What would make him happy? After my Christmas of contrast, I began to think this way with regard to Jesus' birthday. I truly wanted to honor Him. I wanted my celebration to respect His nature and His mission.

It Had to Be Real

The first change to be made was getting rid of the artificial Christmas tree we bought for our little house in Stillwater. I mentioned the house was old and well worn, didn't I? It had deep shag carpet in the living room where the tree would go. As I surveyed the situation, I thought about all the work it would take to keep pine needles from collecting in the carpet. When a discount store put an artificial tree on sale, I reluctantly bought one. I say reluctantly because I'm partial to real trees. It was the practical thing to do.

The first Christmas after the Christmas of contrast, I refused to unpack the artificial tree. It had shed needles just like a real tree. No wonder it was a bargain! But the fact that it was messy was not why I wanted to replace it. It was because the tree looked dead. It had stood lifeless in the corner of my living room as if it were a funeral arrangement ready to be placed on a grave. I worship a living Savior, so I wanted something that reflected His aliveness—which called for a real tree. Its *evergreen* color symbolized that He would live forever. Its fragrance wrapped itself around me as His love does. The aroma permeated my house, calling my thoughts and attention to Him time and time again.

Okay, okay, I realize a cut tree is not really a live tree since it has been cut, but that made it even more symbolic for me. It reminded me how Jesus' earthly life was cut short by His death on a tree, yet His fragrance and His realness live on.

I realize other Marthas may feel differently, because having an artificial tree is certainly sensible. If I were going to use an artificial tree, I could honor Jesus by decorating it with symbolic ornaments that reflect His birth, His life, His teachings, His death, and His resurrection. As we will see in the next chapter, I did this kind of thing with symbols on a flat, felt tree to teach my children about Jesus. The symbols would work just as well on an artificial tree. Or an artificial tree could be decorated with ornaments from around the world, representing Jesus' love for people everywhere and His desire for all people to know Him.

To use a natural tree was—and is—important to me because, as I wrote earlier, God speaks to me through His creative work. The Bible teaches that Jesus was there in the beginning, taking an active role in creation. It seemed to me then that I should show regard for His work by being a good steward of natural resources.

Unwrapping Again and Again

In a time when the planet He created is groaning under the weight of waste, I shouldn't thoughtlessly or carelessly add to that waste. I understand that we all add to it daily just by living, but I mean adding stuff just to have stuff, going to excess in what we buy, and refusing to recycle.

So I use the same decorations year after year. The plus in that is that with each one you unwrap you have wonderful memories to share with those you decorate with. Some are ornaments the children have made. Some are items that have been given to us. I'm still using one that was given to me in college and some from our first tree as a married couple.

Bob and I learned an important lesson about trees that first Christmas. Outside they look much smaller than they do in the house! We were so excited about our first tree. We went to a tree farm where we could choose it and have it cut right before our eyes. We were so proud as we hauled it home—it was going to look so nice in front of our picture window, but alas, we knew we had problems when we put it on the front porch. How were we going to get it inside?

With lots of pushing, we managed to get the tree through the door and in our house, but it almost filled up our little living room. The decorations we had bought didn't begin to cover the whole tree, so we only decorated the front and kept the drapes pulled. My husband's boss's wife, who lived across the way, noticed our closed drapes. When she saw me, she asked, "Don't you two have a Christmas tree?"

"Yes, we have a tree."

"I didn't think you did since your drapes are closed."

I explained, "That's because we don't have enough decorations for our tree."

She said, "I've been sorting my ornaments and getting ready to toss some out. Would you like to have those?"

Of course I said yes. We're still using those decorations she was going to throw away!

Creative Recycling

In addition to using decorations over and over, I also make postcards and gift tags out of used Christmas cards. I reuse gift-wrap and gift bags. For gifts within our immediate family, I use the financial pages of *The Wall Street Journal* and the funnies from the Sunday newspaper. The financial pages look great with a red or green bow. A gold bow works well for the funnies. Our sons have never hesitated to receive a gift wrapped in this manner!

I realize to some Marthas recycling in this way would be depressing, but it isn't when you keep the word *creative* in front of recycling. This puts some fun in the activity when you begin to see what kinds of things you can put together and what kind of look you can create.

Even with reusing and recycling, I realize my efforts are not going make a dent in the local landfill. I still have the sense that I am pleasing Jesus, that I am respecting what He created. I didn't realize how strongly I was coming to feel about this until a Sunday school teacher suggested we spend ten dollars apiece on gag gifts for each other. I said a little too sharply, "You want us to do what?"

I bristled because I didn't want to give a gag gift in the name of Jesus that would add to the clutter at my house and then to the refuse at the landfill. If I were going to spend $20 ($10 for Bob and $10 for me), I would rather give that money to missions.

I didn't want to discourage the teacher, though, with my quick remark, so somewhat more sweetly I suggested a white elephant gift exchange. A white elephant is something of value you have at your home but is not valuable to you, yet it is too good to throw away. She responded favorably to my suggestion, and we had a fun time exchanging white elephants. A few years later I designed a whole party around the idea, only I called it a "green elephant" party. The word green, of course, means environmentally friendly—saving those precious trees God created. And, of course, I requested that the gifts be wrapped in recycled paper!

Entertaining His Way

In addition to using a natural tree, reusing decorations, and creatively recycling to honor Jesus, I also tried to entertain in a way that reflected Him. I kept things simple and uncluttered and yet in good taste. I used nativity scenes that friends in the faith had given me. I welcomed people into my home with respect and warmth. I tried to find things for everyone to do to make them feel comfortable and accepted. Of course, when you make an effort to reflect someone else, that doesn't mean others will always recognize it. What was important, of course, was that Jesus was pleased, but still it was nice when Ron, a frequent guest at our Christmas celebrations, appeared to see what I was about.

My mother had made and given me a quilted wall hanging with a Santa in the middle saying "Bah, humbug!" I hung it because she gave it to me and I felt I should. When I saw Ron studying it, I walked up to him. He turned and said, "This is not you, Brenda." It truly wasn't. I put the wall hanging away not to use it again. I keep it because my mother made it, but it is not a part of my Christmas decorations because it doesn't appropriately reflect my feelings or my attitude. What I need is a wall hanging that says, "Happy Birthday, Jesus!"

Chapter 12

WISE WOMEN FOLLOW THE WISE MEN

Even though the plaque was one of many items on the wall of the garage, I couldn't help but notice it while waiting for my car to be repaired. It was white with holly painted on it and a red ribbon glued to the corner, so it stood out among the grease-covered certificates, reminders, cute sayings, and "no checks accepted" signs. The plaque said: "Three *wise* men…are you serious?"

I knew the secretaries must have hung it there because when the mechanic went to figure my bill, he said, "The 'girls' aren't here, so I don't know if I am doing this right." His words reminded me of a joke that circulated on the Internet several Christmases ago. Numerous people forwarded it to me.

Do you know what would have happened if it had been three wise women instead of three wise men? They would have asked

directions, arrived on time, helped deliver the baby, cleaned the
stable, made a casserole, and brought practical gifts.

While we poke fun at the wise men, they were truly wise in a way that women who want a Mary Christmas might want to emulate. They were earnest learners who pursued the truth.

Students of the Stars

Much mystery surrounds the wise men. Who were they really? The tradition that they were kings probably grew out of a messianic prophecy from Psalm 68:29: "Because of your temple at Jerusalem kings will bring you gifts" (NIV). Matthew, who tells their story, does not say they were kings.

More probably they were astrologers and philosophers who advised kings. As astrologers, they studied the sky, taking note of stars, formations, patterns, and movement. They pondered what they saw, made interpretations and speculations. They believed that they could foretell the future from the stars, and they believed that a man's destiny was settled by the star under which he was born.

As philosophers, they would have also had an interest in what was happening around them, what was being said, and what people were expecting in the future. They could "put two and two together"—what they saw in the heavens with what they heard and observed on earth. They were aware, for example, that the Jews were expecting a king. This expectation began with Jewish prophets and eventually spread beyond Palestine until it became common knowledge among the Gentiles.

When an out-of-the-ordinary star appeared, the wise men wondered if the time wasn't right for the Jewish king to appear. They determined to find out by investigating and pursuing the truth.

Naturally, they headed to Jerusalem to see Herod, the current ruler of the Jews. They asked him, "Where is the one who has been born king of the Jews? We saw his star in the east and have come to worship him" (Matthew 2:2 NIV).

King Herod, a wicked man and a tight ruler, asked questions of the chief priests, the teachers of the law, and the wise men. Asking questions is often indicative of someone who is seeking truth, but this wasn't Herod's motive. He was disturbed by the possibility that a king of the Jews had been born—someone who might replace him—so he didn't say to the wise men, "Let me go with you so that I may worship the King."

Because Herod was troubled, the Jewish people were, too, but they didn't follow the wise men either, even though they had been waiting for the king of the Jews to be born.

The wise men pursued their search; they went on to Bethlehem and were rewarded. The star they had seen in the east reappeared. It went ahead of them until it stopped over the place where Jesus was.

When they saw the star, they were overjoyed. What a great reward for their pursuit! What marvelous confirmation for them of God's leading! They couldn't help but respond in adoration. "On coming to the house, they saw the child with his mother Mary, and they bowed down and worshiped him. Then they opened their treasures and presented him with gifts of gold and of incense and of myrrh" (Matthew 2:11 NIV).

Many people must have seen the unusual star, but only the wise men pursued its meaning. By their honest searching, the wise men were able to perceive and to experience what others missed. Using their minds was a key to their spiritual perception, and it could be to ours as well.

With All Your Mind

The Bible says, "Love the Lord your God with all your heart and with all your soul and *with all your mind*" (Matthew 22:37 NIV, emphasis mine). When Mary sat at Jesus' feet, she was loving Him with her heart, but she was also loving Him with her mind as she listened to Him. An engaged mind is an alert mind; an engaged mind is a focused mind. Focus and alertness strengthen spiritual perception and increase spiritual receptivity.

I connected using the mind with having a Mary Christmas when I developed an advent emphasis for my sons. I was a schoolteacher before I married, so I had noticed that once the Christmas decorations are up, children seem to be ready for something to occur. I wondered if my sons weren't ready to learn. *Maybe we could do something that focused on Jesus each day.*

After much thought and with the help of a friend, I developed 25 devotionals beginning with Jesus' birth and continuing through His resurrection. We made a corresponding felt symbol for each. Thankfully, no sewing was involved! We made the symbols out of brightly-colored felt scraps, and each day a family member placed a felt symbol on a green felt tree that we hung by the breakfast table.

We had symbols for the birth of Jesus (manger), the visitation of the shepherds (shepherd's crook), and the wise men (a star), but we also had the dove for His baptism, a boat for His preaching to people on shore, a lamp for His being the light of the world, a crown for the crown of thorns, a cross for His death, and a butterfly for His resurrection. With the daily emphasis, we celebrated Jesus' life and death as well as His birth.

Beginning December 1 and continuing each day through Christmas Day, one of our sons placed a symbol on the tree while my husband or I explained its significance. Eventually the boys took turns explaining the symbols.

As I studied the life of Christ to develop this activity, I noticed something happen that frequently happens when I study the Bible. I sensed His presence and I learned from Him. He became my Teacher.

I've often heard people say that devotional reading of the Bible and studying the Bible are two different things. When you are having devotions, you feel personal and close to God. When you are studying, you are gathering facts and learning information. That hasn't been my experience. God speaks to me through both, but it's more often that He speaks to me when I am studying than when I doing devotional reading. I think it is because I focus more, engage my mind, and increase my alertness. That's why after developing the life of Christ emphasis for my children, I began to look for other ways to expand my mind at Christmas.

Being a Learner

During December, to sit at His feet, to be a learner, I prefer to chew on something a little out of the ordinary. Some Christmases, I have read a whole Gospel in one sitting rather than just the portions of Luke and Matthew where Jesus' birth story is told. This gave me a broader picture of Jesus' life and helped me to know Him better. Something else I liked to do was to study a passage that connects to Christmas but is not repeated year after year as Luke 2 and portions of Matthew 1–2 are. John 1, where God's becoming flesh is emphasized, is rich study. I also like John's recognition of Jesus' humanity in his first letter. A study of Jesus' "I am" statements in John's Gospel was also insightful and enriching.

I wouldn't be a true Martha, though, if I didn't admit that studying is something I can easily let slide to the bottom of my list of priorities when preparing for Christmas. That's when I have to remember that the wise men were *disciplined* learners; I have to make myself find the time. Offering to teach Sunday school helps. It becomes the star that guides my study as I look for truths. I still remember the year I had to teach the "begats" of Matthew to a small class. The penciled notes for how to pronounce all the names are still in my Bible! I'll admit I groaned at first—*this is going to be so dull!* But through disciplined study God opened up new vistas and insights to me as He does so well when we open our minds and seek the truth.

Disciplined study not only makes me more spiritually aware, it improves my ability to recognize Him when He appears. If we want a Mary Christmas, we need to be able to identify Him. The real Jesus is not going to appear to us as a baby.

Last Christmas, in a worship service I was attending, the minister invited the worshipers to reach out to the Christ child and to seek His presence and His help. I thought, *That's not right. He is no longer a baby in a manger or even a child.* The one we want to experience, the one at whose feet we want to sit, is our crucified and risen Lord. He is the one who can and will respond to us, and so we need to be able to recognize Him. We don't want to miss Him like Herod or all the other people who saw the star but didn't use their minds to look for the truth.

Chapter 13

DID JESUS GET CHIGGERS?

What woman doesn't think about where she will put the Christmas tree when looking at a house to buy? I know I always did in our various moves. I even thought about where I would put the cardboard nativity scene that Jim and Joel played with and learned from in Stillwater. With the crèche, I had helped them understand that Jesus was real—this was important to me after my experience as a child. There are so many fantasy characters attached to Christmas, I wanted to make sure my children knew Jesus was real and not a made-up person.

I enjoyed using the nativity scene with Jim and Joel so much—and felt they gained from the experience—that I looked forward to sharing it with our new son Ben. When we were looking for a house in Broken Arrow, Oklahoma, I was cuddling eight-month-old Ben in my arms and thinking about "next Christmas" when he would, I thought, be just the right age for introducing him to Jesus' birth story.

In one house, I spied a low kitchen shelf on a wide divider between the kitchen and the dining room. It was at the eye level of a two-year-old. I don't know what past residents might have used the shelf for, but I saw it as the right spot for the nativity scene. Immediately in my mind's eye I saw myself teaching Ben. I would stir soup at the stove, which was in the divider, while Ben played nearby with Mary, Joseph, the wise men, and the shepherds. I would tell him the story of baby Jesus and we would have conversations about it. I beamed at the thought of memorable moments together.

So we bought the house. Okay, I'll admit, we made the decision based on more than where the nativity scene would go! The next Christmas, when Ben was twenty months old, I displayed the cardboard crèche on the low kitchen shelf and waited with expectancy.

Ben's Reaction

When Ben saw the crèche, his eyes lit up, and I opened my mouth to tell the story. Ben, though, had other plans. He marched up to the counter, reached out his arm, and in one wide sweep wiped the crèche off the counter.

"No, Ben! You mustn't do that to baby Jesus," I explained patiently. I tried to tell the Christmas story to Ben as I picked up the figures, but he wouldn't listen. He was off to find Pluto, a large plastic dog he rode in the house.

I picked up the figures and arranged them back on the ledge while Ben on Pluto circled through the house. Soon he was back. Again, he wiped off the nativity scene with Mary, Joseph, and baby Jesus falling to the floor. Not quite as patiently this time, I said, "No, no, Ben, you mustn't do that to baby Jesus." I tried to tell the story of Jesus' birth as I picked up the pieces, but he refused to listen.

I thought Ben would soon tire of wiping the figures off the ledge, and then I could get on with telling the story. Ben, though, wouldn't stop long enough to listen. All he wanted to do was ride Pluto.

The next time Ben stopped to look he didn't even get off Pluto. With one fell swoop, he knocked the figures off. I said—impatiently this time—"No, no, Ben, you mustn't do that to baby Jesus." Ben didn't hear what I said, but I did, and I didn't like what I heard. I heard "no, no" and "Jesus" in the same sentence. Did those two go together? Did I want my child's early association with the name of Jesus to be negative? No, I didn't, so I put the crèche away to save for when Ben was older, but I wished there were something Ben and I could do together to emphasize the realness of Jesus. Jim and Joel were in school every day, so Ben and I had a lot of time together in a house whose decorations indicated that something significant was happening. What could we do?

Why Not a Manger

One day, as I rocked Ben to sleep for his nap, I prayed, "Father, if there is some way that I can relate Your Son to Ben, please show me." That evening I attended a Christmas program where the participants acted out the events of Bethlehem. When Mary tenderly held baby Jesus and then laid Him in the manger, I thought of the times I cuddled Ben and then put him to bed. *Ben understood babies, I thought. Why not a real manger?*

I asked my husband to build a manger. Bob looked at me like I was crazy, but to please me he constructed a wooden feeding trough from some very weathered boards—so weathered we labeled the manger "authentic Bethlehem." Bob put straw in it and set it by the Christmas tree. I took a baby doll, wrapped it in "swaddling clothes" and laid it in the manger.

When Ben saw the manger, his eyes lit up...like they had when he saw the cardboard nativity scene...so I held my breath. I waited to see what he would do.

This time Ben went to the baby Jesus doll, picked him up, put him over his shoulder, and patted him. As Ben loved on the baby, I saw my opportunity. I said, "Jesus loves Ben." A short while later Ben was back to cuddle the baby. Again I said, "Jesus loves Ben."

Over and over in the days before Christmas, Ben picked up baby Jesus and loved him. Each time, I affirmed Jesus' love for him. Sometimes I stopped what I was doing and patted Ben while he patted the doll. I've noticed that when you help your children grasp Jesus, you grasp Him too. As I spoke of Jesus' love to Ben I was also warmed by His love. I knew He was right there with us.

At Ben's insistence, we continued for several years to use the manger with a baby doll beside our lighted Christmas tree.

Each year when Ben and I took the manger out of storage, Ben always had questions. "Did Jesus grow up?" "Was Jesus a little boy like me?" "What happened to Jesus?" "Where is He now?"

One year when we brushed the bugs and cobwebs off the manger before bringing it into the house, Ben asked, "Did Jesus get chiggers?" I knew then that Ben was indeed grasping the reality of Jesus' birth. I could hear the wheels turning in his little mind: If His birth took place outside, if it was in a stable where animals were kept, then how could you lay a baby in a feeding trough? Isn't that where the animals ate? Wouldn't bugs get on him? He was grasping the reality of a biblical truth: "The Word was made flesh, and dwelt among us" (John 1:14 KJV).

Chapter 14

FILLING
$\mathcal{H}$EART-BASKETS

I once read about a family who placed two baskets in their living room during December. One basket contained a bundle of straw, the other a figure of baby Jesus. Every time one of the family members treated another with special kindness, the recipient of the kind act transferred a small bit of straw to the basket where baby Jesus was. By the time Christmas Day came, acts of kindness had made the baby's bed soft with straw.

I've held this story in my mind as I've written about reflecting, simplifying, and learning. It gave me a picture to work with as I tried to describe what we are doing when we take time to be quiet, to simplify our celebration, or to study about Jesus. We are readying an inner place of spiritual receptivity or, we might say, preparing a heart-basket.

We've been learning from the shepherds and the wise men how to do this, and we can also learn from

Simeon and Anna, two individuals whose heart-baskets were well padded. They had worshiped God for a very long time and were more than ready to receive His Son.

A Very Special Baby

After Jesus was 41 days old, Mary and Joseph took Him "to Jerusalem to present him to the Lord" (Luke 2:22b). Their main reason for going was to participate in the Redemption of the Firstborn ceremony and to complete Mary's purification rite at the temple, but a little parental pride might have also been involved. Many parents of newborns want to take their babies to church to show them off and to hear people ooh and ah over the baby. If that were the case with Mary and Joseph, they were not disappointed.

Two old people, Simeon and Anna, who regularly "hung out" at the temple, shared in their joy and let Joseph and Mary know just how unusual their son was.

Simeon took Jesus in his arms and praised God, "Now, Lord.... With my own eyes I have seen your salvation, which you have prepared in the presence of all peoples: A light to reveal your will to the Gentiles and bring glory to your people Israel" (Luke 2:29–32).

Mary and Joseph were amazed at what Simeon said. Of course, most parents believe their child is special, but Mary and Joseph already had strong indications that their son was. There was the appearance of the angel Gabriel to Mary, the dreams Joseph received, and the visitations of the shepherds and the wise men, but one thing they had probably not connected Jesus with was Gentiles. Simeon said their child would be a revealing light to the Gentiles as well as a redeeming glory to Jews. Their child was destined for unusual things. Wow!

Anna, too, delighted in the child. She gave thanks to God and spoke about Him to others who were looking for the redemption of Jerusalem. "See this baby. He's going to grow up and set Jerusalem free. This little baby is who we have been looking for. Here in my arms is the answer to our concerns!"

Up to this point, you may not see anything remarkable about the response of Simeon and Anna. Old people usually make over babies, often in very glowing words, but these two recognized *baby* Jesus as the Messiah, the deliverer the Jews were looking for. The Jews, though, weren't expecting a baby!

As God's chosen people, the Jews believed they were destined for greatness, and being subservient to the Romans, who were currently in control, didn't fit the picture. They believed that someday they would be in charge. For that to come about, many believed some great champion would descend upon the earth. He would be like King David and revive all of the nation's old glories when God's people were united and powerful under David's leadership. They certainly never thought of the deliverer in terms of a tiny baby. They saw him as a rich and powerful man who would descend upon the earth, deliver them from the Romans, and put the Jews back in control. So how was it that Simeon and Anna recognized baby Jesus as being the promised Messiah? They had been shaped by a lifetime of worship.

Shaped by a Lifetime

Simeon was a righteous and devout man who expectantly and prayerfully looked for "the consolation of Israel," their messianic deliverer. The Holy Spirit was upon Simeon and had assured him that he would not die before he had seen the Messiah. On the day when Mary and Joseph came with baby Jesus to the temple, Simeon was moved by the Spirit to be there. Many people came and went, but the Holy Spirit connected these four.

For years and years, Simeon waited quietly and patiently upon God. In humble and faithful expectation, he waited for the day when God would comfort His people. He was confident his life would not end until he had seen God's Anointed One. In baby Jesus he recognized the Messiah and was glad. Now he was ready to die in peace.

Anna was a very old prophetess, a widow who had only had seven years with her husband before he died. She was now 84 years old and during all this time she had never ceased to hope. So devoted was she that she never left the Temple; day and night she worshiped God, fasting and praying.

What happened in the lives of Simeon and Anna is what always happens in the process of worship; you become more and more like the object of your worship. Therefore, when this manifestation of

God's salvation came to their attention, they knew who He was. They had so identified their affections with God that they were able to recognize what others saw but did not perceive.

Simeon and Anna's example is not saying we have to be old to have a heart-basket ready to receive Jesus! Age may help, but it can also be a detriment.

When Wonder Dies

Sometimes the things that happen to us in life can chip away at our sense of wonder and our believing faith. We may become cynical or grimly resigned to things as they are. We may lose our tender side where we are easily touched or moved. If that had happened to Simeon and Anna and someone asked them, "Do you expect to see the promised Messiah?" they would have answered "Not in my lifetime!"

But that's not what happened to Simeon and Anna. Simeon held on to a promise the way a child would. "You promised, Mom, that you would take us to the zoo on Friday if it doesn't rain. Remember, Mom? You promised." "Dad, you said if I swept the garage and cleaned my room, you would pay me ten dollars. You meant that, didn't you? I've got the garage swept now and my room clean. Well, Dad?" Through the years, through devoted worship, Simeon kept his childlike faith.

Anna held on even when her heart was broken, when love and laughter were snatched away from her at a young age when her husband died. She could have grieved her heart away, held it against God, and mourned for the children she never had. But she didn't. She let go of her sorrow, gave it to God, and worshiped Him. In the process, she came to know God so well that when she held His Son in her arms, she knew who He was.

The example of Simeon and Anna reminds us that worship makes excellent "straw" for cushioning our heart-baskets to receive Jesus. Worship softens our hearts, making us spiritually sensitive. Worship recognizes the attributes of God so we can recognize His Son when He appears to us. True worship keeps our sense of wonder and expectancy alive. This may not be encouraging news for some Marthas. With so much on our minds, it can be hard for us to maintain the mental focus worship requires. I've found it hard to concentrate at different times. I've learned, though, that occasional lapses do not prevent me from padding my heart-basket with worship.

Filling My Basket

Simeon and Anna's recognition of Jesus came when they were in a place of worship, but their worship began long before that moment. How I worship in May, July, and September will pad my heart, preparing a place to receive Jesus in December. It is continuous worship that provides Him a rich place to dwell, not a one-time experience. If my personal effort on a particular Sunday morning may not be the best, a Sunday night or the next Sunday morning may be.

My appreciation for Him and my ability to recognize Him have already been nurtured throughout the year.

I also remind myself that worship occurs at other times besides a Sunday morning worship service. It can be during quiet prayers when I seek moments of solitude, it can be part of acts of service when I minister to a needy person, and it can even occur in times of study. Mary sat at Jesus' feet, a position of worship, but she was still learning and interacting with Jesus. All three were intertwined together. The important thing is that the adoration, honor, reverence, and respect due Him are present. I can give Him those things when scrubbing the kitchen floor.

I'm probably the only woman left in America who gets down on her knees (a position of worship!) to mop her floor. I move out the table and chairs, get my bucket of water and cleaning rag, pop in a CD of beautiful Christmas music—music invoking praise and honor—and sing along while I mop. Before I know it, I'm pausing in the middle of the floor and having a precious time talking with Jesus. He responds and reveals Himself giving me a midnight clear moment even if it is only three o'clock in the afternoon. And for that moment, I'm transfigured. I'm no longer Martha making a list of things to do; I'm Mary basking in the presence of Jesus. I'm glad I padded my heart-basket with worship.

Chapter 15

THE MOTHER
WHO STOLE
CHRISTMAS

After looking at the importance of solitude, simplicity, study, and worship, you could get the impression that contrition, somberness, or asceticism are what's necessary to having a Mary Christmas; to have spiritual encounters, we should do away with the celebrative aspects of the holiday.

Through the centuries, many people have concluded that celebrating Christmas does not belong in the life of a believer. Penance or austerity would be more appropriate. Indeed, Advent, the season of spiritual preparation that many Christians observe, began as a period of penance in the fourth century.

Later in history, the Puritans refused to celebrate Christmas. In the early days of our country, they would not allow so much as a mincemeat pie on Christmas day.

Both contrition and asceticism have spiritual merit, but I've also learned that celebration does too. From an austere Christmas that our family experienced, I learned that celebration can also be an avenue for experiencing a Mary Christmas.

The Christmas Damper

"Don't expect much" regularly popped out of my mouth the year my husband had been unemployed for six months. Bob had resumed working in November, but he hadn't been working long enough for us to get caught up on our bills. Not wanting to add to our debt, we decided to spend very little for Christmas.

We bought a marked-down live Christmas tree with a very crooked trunk for ten dollars. We weren't so poor that we were going back to an artificial tree!

While our sons—Jim, Joel, and Ben, ages 13, 12, and 6 at the time—decorated it, they began talking about the gifts they'd open from Bob and me on Christmas morning. *Hmm*, I thought, *I had better nip this anticipation in the bud*. I said, "Now, boys, don't expect much for Christmas this year."

When they saw TV commercials especially designed to make children "want," they dreamed aloud about what they would get. I interrupted their dreams with, "Remember, boys, don't expect much this Christmas."

When Ben's friend, Bruce, came over to play one day, they chatted about the toys they wanted for Christmas as they played. When Bruce left, I said, "Now, Ben, don't expect much for Christmas."

I said "don't expect much" so many times, I felt as if I were becoming a new Christmas character, one to rival Ebenezer Scrooge or the Grinch. I was the Christmas Damper, the dreaded woman who threw water on boys and girls when she heard them expressing their Christmas wishes. Her goal was to put out the fires of Christmas expectation.

A Christmas gloom settled over our house. Jim began spending a lot of time in his room with the door closed. Joel became listless, and hovered over me while I worked at my desk. Ben acted babyish, repeatedly asking if he could sit on my lap.

In November, if anyone had told me this would happen, I'd have said, "Not at my house." I had been certain having little money wouldn't affect our celebration because of the spiritual activities we did together. This year, though, our daily devotions and the manger with baby Jesus held no interest.

When our pastor preached a sermon blaming the loss of meaning on the hustle and bustle of Christmas, I said under my breath, "Bah! Humbug!" I hadn't bought one ribbon, one gift tag, or one piece of wrapping paper. We weren't caught up in the hustle and bustle of the holidays, but something was missing from our Christmas.

I was relieved when a real estate agent that I sometimes worked for called. Carileen said, "I've decided to have an open house. I want to show my new home to my customers. Would you bake the cookies, prepare the punch and then serve them at my open house?"

I welcomed the job. *Perhaps baking 30 dozen cookies and preparing punch will get my thoughts off our gloomy Christmas.* It did while I shopped for the ingredients. But when

I rolled the dough for the sugar cookies, I thought of my mother, five hundred miles away. At that moment, she was probably also baking. During the holidays, people came and went at Mother's house, and she offered pie and coffee to each one. Warmth permeated her home. I began to wonder how my mother achieved that holiday warmth. How did she create an atmosphere in which people felt comfortable stopping by without being asked? Did it take years of living in a community? Did it happen only when relatives lived nearby? Our family had no relatives close by, and we hadn't lived in our community long. Thinking about the warmth in my mother's home made the Christmas gloom hang even heavier.

The morning of Carileen's open house, I wrote in my journal, "There's something wrong with this Christmas. Sadness prevails. My family is not excited or happy about Christmas, yet I don't want it to be this way. I want something more because Christmas is significant."

"Lord Jesus," I prayed, "I have always tried to honor you at Christmas. Help me to identify what the problem is and help me see how to correct it."

I loaded the cookies, the serving trays, the punch, and the punch bowl and went to Carileen's. I kept the punch bowl filled and cookies on the trays while her customers came and went. As I listened to their happy chatter, I felt a warmth similar to that at my mother's house. At Mother's, people came and went because they knew her. At Carileen's, people came and went because they were invited. If I wanted to create warmth at my own home, perhaps I needed to invite people, too.

Let's Do It

When I got home, I took a deep breath and said to Bob and the boys, "I have an idea. I know this sounds crazy, but let's have an open house."

"No one would come," Bob said. "Everyone we know will be spending Christmas with their families."

"Perhaps we could ask them to stop by Christmas Eve afternoon for a few minutes on the way to wherever they are going," I countered.

"But you have been reminding us all month how little money we have. How can we afford an open house?" asked Jim, his anger clearly evident.

"People won't eat much if they're on their way to some place where they'll be eating. Besides, I learned this week that a five-pound sack of flour makes a lot of cookies. We could serve cookies and punch. Instead of an elaborate fruit punch, I could serve that Kool-Aid and orange juice combination I make for you in the summer."

"What about postage?" said Bob.

I responded. "Let's hand-deliver them! We could pass them out at church tomorrow, and you kids can take them to school. You can invite whomever you want."

When I said that, their eyes lit up. Together, they said, "Let's do it."

"I'll need your help if we are going to get everything ready in time."

Bob, our resident poet, said, "I'll make the invitations. A poem is already forming in my head."

We gave out invitations at church the next day, and the boys took them to school on Monday. What fun we had handing out invitations to people we knew well, to people we wanted to know better, and to people in situations like ours!

On Monday and Tuesday after school, we baked cookies. On Wednesday, with no school, Jim, Joel, Ben, and I cleaned house. The weather was unseasonably warm, so we opened the windows. We polished the furniture with lemon oil and shook the rugs. Anyone driving by our country home would have thought spring-cleaning was taking place!

Finally, thirty minutes before time for the open house to begin on Thursday, we had everything ready. The boys kept opening the front door to look down the road to see if anyone was coming. After several looks, they sat down. Joel said, "Can you believe it? Can you believe we finally have everything ready?"

And then I had a midnight clear moment. Jesus came in the fullness of time when God had everything ready (Galatians 4:4). I said, "God, the Father, planned and made special arrangements for Jesus' birth. God picked out a name. He chose a birthplace. He prepared the people by promising them from time to time that Jesus would come. Now that we understand what it takes to get ready for something important, let's thank God for preparing the world for Jesus' coming."

We said our prayer, and the doorbell rang. The first guest had arrived! During the afternoon 37 people came—just the right number. Their coming and going stretched out over the afternoon so there was lots of leisurely conversation. And with each new visitor to our home came a warmth that lingered long after the last guest departed.

The gloom had departed earlier. From the time we started planning our open house, the boys no longer talked about what they were going to *get* for Christmas. Gifts no longer mattered. In a year when we didn't have much, we learned that celebration matters.

Celebration's Value

Intrigued, I began studying celebration and learned how vital it is to the sustenance of the human spirit. The history of Christmas bears this out. Winter festivals involving fires and evergreens were in existence long before Christians decided to celebrate Christ's birth in the winter. People had an ineradicable need for some sort of light in the long cold dark. The burst of light and the need to feast permeate the annals of history.

People need a bright spot to get them through winter, and celebrating can provide that needed brightness. Holidays provide a break from routine. Special days give us an excuse to put worries, cares, and goals on hold. Although the Puritans would have nothing to do with Christmas, they still felt the need to offer thanksgiving. Community and congregational thanksgiving days were declared for special causes: the end of an epidemic, rainfall after a drought, and victory in war. These thanksgiving days were days of prayer followed by "making merry" at family dinners where mincemeat pie became a part of the menu!

Chapter 16

LET'S GO SEE

When one of our grandchildren came to live with us, he was three and a half and could only speak French. One of the first English phrases he learned was "Let's go." That's probably because his grandparents often used the phrase. When we wanted to go upstairs, go downstairs, go outside, go for a ride, take a walk, or just move from room to room, we said, "Let's go." Christophe's dark little eyes would light up in eager anticipation. He was ready to act.

The shepherds and the wise men had this same kind of eagerness. They were participants in the drama of life, not spectators or casual observers. They responded to what they experienced by taking action.

Let's Go to Bethlehem

The appearance of the angel of the Lord to the shepherds was very unusual. This was not an everyday occurrence, so that alone would have been marvelous, but the glory of the Lord also shone around them. We don't know how the Lord's glory revealed itself, but we do know it terrified the shepherds (Luke 2:9). Recognizing their fear, the angel said to them, "Do not be afraid. I bring you good news of great joy that will be for all the people. Today in the town of David a Savior has been born to you; he is Christ the Lord. This will be a sign to you: You will find a baby wrapped in cloths and lying in a manger" (Luke 2:10–12 NIV). Then a great host of angels joined in, and all of them praised God together.

What did the shepherds do after experiencing this spectacular event? Did they say, "Interesting sight, wasn't it? Wasn't it nice of God to send an angel to tell us the Messiah is here? I wish we could go to Bethlehem, but we have the sheep to look after."

No, they didn't say that. Instead, they said to one another, *"Let's go.* Let's go to Bethlehem and see this thing that has happened." What they saw and what they heard could not be ignored. They had to act, "so they hurried off and found Mary and Joseph, and the baby, who was lying in the manger" (Luke 2:16 NIV).

Something very unusual and meaningful was happening, and the shepherds just had to respond. So did the wise men when they saw the star.

Let's Follow the Star

From their lifetime of learning, the wise men knew an unusual star meant something, perhaps the birth of a king. When they saw the extraordinary star over Bethlehem, they said to one another, "Let's go. Let's follow the star and see where it leads us."

I'm certain other astrologers were also scanning the night sky and saw the same star but they didn't pursue it. Their conversation might have gone like this.

"Say, did you see that unusual star?"

"I sure did. What do you think it means?"

"Probably represents a king being born somewhere. Say, isn't there some kind of folklore or something that says that a great king will be born to the Jews?"

"Yes, I think there is...you may be on to something."

"Regardless, it was nice seeing an unusual star tonight. It's not every night that you get to see a star like this. Well, I think I'm about ready to head for bed. How about you?"

Yawn. "Good night."

The wise men, though, said to each other, *"Let's go. Let's go investigate. Let's find out what is happening."*

Can't you feel their excitement as they got on their camels and headed out to follow the star? They didn't know where they were going or exactly what they were going to find, but they couldn't help themselves. Their action was a celebration of what they had seen and heard, something most of us understand.

Let's Respond

If you've ever graduated from high school, been promoted, had a baby, been rescued from a troubling situation, finished basic training, received an award for outstanding sales, or been given a clean bill of health, you can understand the emotions the shepherds and the wise men were experiencing. You feel like lighting sparklers, kicking your feet in the air, having a party, or calling your friends. You've just got to do something, even if it is just sharing the good news with someone!

Ideally, that's the feeling we would like to come to Christmas with, to be excited about Jesus' birth and eager to celebrate. Christmas for us, though, doesn't have the newness or fascination that it did for the shepherds and the wise men. We do Christmas every year and we know well why we are celebrating. Instead of wanting to light sparklers, you may feel like someone needs to light a fire under you. Instead of wanting to kick your heels together, you may wish you could cover your head and resurface after January 2. What you are experiencing is a malady that I call *Merry Christmas Resistance*. I know because I've had it several times.

Let's Not Resist

Even after experiencing many Mary Christmases and walking closely with Jesus, I occasionally find myself resisting celebrating His birth. I'm just not ready to prepare for Christmas *again*. It seems like I just finished putting away the decorations from last Christmas.

Occasionally I've been so involved in a project or planning a retreat that I don't want to change focus. I've also resisted Christmas when I've been sad or blue. Other events of our lives don't always synchronize themselves so all will be swell at Christmas—

events like having your husband finally find employ-
ment (the year of our open house), moving to a new
house (yes, I've moved in December—with a baby
who had pneumonia!), having an automobile accident
(14 days in the hospital in December!), or experiencing loss (my mother-in-law died in December). Sometimes you would rather pull the shades down than
light up a tree.

Some women can't get in the mood to celebrate
because of having to make so many decisions regarding
gifts and entertaining. While writing this book, I came
upon a woman breathing hard in the dishtowel/pot
holder section of Wal-Mart. As I reached for some bargain dishcloths, I noticed her picking up one and then
another kind of dishtowel as if some major decision
was hanging in the balance. I thought, *I'll bet she's a
Martha.* I took a chance. "Are you having a hard time
making a decision?"

"Yes," she sighed, "I can't decide which ones to get.
I'm trying to find some dishtowels for my mother-in-
law, but I just don't know which ones she would like."

"Kind of hard, isn't it?"

"Well, my husband is the one who should be picking these out. It's his mother. But he refuses. He says,
'No, you do it.'"

And then she said those words that are symptomatic
of Marthas who have Merry Christmas Resistance.
She said, "I'll be glad when Christmas is over."

I understand this kind of resistance. It makes you
want to do nothing, but interestingly, the antidote is
doing something.

Let's Act

I've found that if I take some kind of action (even if I have to make myself) and respond to what I know is true instead of how I feel, then my resistance melts. Once I decide to commit myself in some way—once I become a "let's go" type of person—something changes within me. Some kind of inner key turns, changing my gloom to joy like it did when our family began planning our open house.

When I step into an active role, I get excited and the celebration becomes *mine* instead of theirs. It becomes my response to Jesus' realness. I cease being a spectator and become an involved participant. One year, as I said, I turned the key by planning our open house. I've also turned the key by planning programs for nursing home residents, agreeing to be a narrator for a Christmas cantata, planning a surprise for someone, deciding to have a party, or inviting someone for a meal.

What I learned is when that inner key starts to turn, I begin preparing a fresh lining for my heart-basket. I prepare for and anticipate a visit from Jesus.

Let's See Jesus

After they arrived in Bethlehem, the shepherds saw everything just as the angel said. What verification for them that God truly was acting! The feeling of wanting to light sparklers cascaded into fireworks, and they couldn't help but respond again and again.

They spread the word. They talked about the baby and the visitation of the angel of the Lord and the heavenly host to all who would listen. When they got back to the fields, they glorified and praised God.

In pursuing the king the star represented, the wise men went to Jerusalem, and the star disappeared from their sight for a while. They asked questions and learned the King of the Jews would be born in Bethlehem, so they went on and were rewarded. The star returned and stopped over the place where Jesus was. When they saw the star, they were overjoyed. When they saw Jesus with his mother Mary, they bowed down and worshiped Him. Then they opened their treasures and presented him with gifts of gold and of incense and of myrrh.

When we act in light of what we know to be true, expectations are aroused. We begin to look for Him and anticipate His appearance, and He reveals Himself. Having a Mary Christmas doesn't mean having to always be quiet or meditative. It doesn't mean there's never any rushing and that everything is well planned and runs smoothly with time for hour-long devotions every day. It means seeing Jesus, listening to Him, learning from Him, and interacting with Him. This can be done through celebrating just as it can be through quietness, simplicity, learning, and worship. So when we are struck with Merry Christmas Resistance, let's go. Let's go call a friend or two, bake a cake, and celebrate!

Chapter 17

WE DREW
A CIRCLE
THAT TOOK
*H*IM IN

C elebration gives us a channel to be blessed or to bless others. Celebrating reaches out to people and pulls them in where they can experience Jesus' love, warmth, and acceptance. I was reminded of this when Ruby came to our open house.

Lonely Eyes Connect

Ruby and her husband Thom were even newer to our community than our family, so naturally I invited them. But I didn't think they would come. They were sure to be busy on Christmas Eve because they were gregarious, outgoing people. At the Wednesday night church suppers, I noticed the way they laughed and mingled easily with others.

But they did come. Thom quickly filled his plate in the dining room and headed for the conversation in the family room. Ruby lingered behind watching me fill plates with cookies.

She said, "I didn't know you were lonely."

"What?"

"Your invitation. It said you were lonely. I thought I was the only one."

I remembered then what Bob had said in his poem: "On the day before Christmas, Brenda gets lonesome and blue. And the Poinsett men know not what to do! This year will be different—with your help, tears we'll dry. If, for a minute or two, you'll kindly stop by."

I started to protest and tell her Bob only said that because I had a touch of the Christmas blues. But I saw loneliness in her eyes, so I simply said, "You, too?"

"Yes," she said, and at that moment, memories of the beautifully presented foods Ruby brought to our church's fellowship meals flashed through my mind. I remembered marveling at how good they were to look at and to taste. She had been a chef in another city, and now her job was in the elementary school cafeteria, where everything was done simply and uniformly. What a difficult adjustment her move must have been for her! She must have felt stifled to leave behind her creative outlet. She was not only missing family and friends but she was missing a part of herself.

I reached out and hugged Ruby and together we shared the comfort of acknowledging our feelings of loneliness. I determined to include her and Thom in any future celebrations.

Lonely Eyes See the Glory

My husband and I taught a Sunday school class of single adults and from time to time we had get-togethers. In February we planned a Mexican meal, so I invited Thom and Ruby to join us. Obviously, they weren't single, but I knew our group would appreciate Ruby's culinary delights. Ruby readily accepted our invitation and agreed to bring enchiladas!

The day of the get-together we had a huge snowstorm. It was a beautiful snow—the kind of moist, heavy snow that clings to pine needles—the kind you dream about for a white Christmas. The snow stopped in the late afternoon, so for city dwellers it would not have interfered with a party; snowplows would have quickly cleared the streets. But we lived in the country, where there was no snow removal. Plus we lived on a dirt road with a steep hill to traverse before getting to our house. I wondered if anyone would come, but our class members tended to have a "let's go" attitude. They piled into trucks and came anyway in that cold, clear night. Thom and Ruby came too, bringing two big pans of enchiladas.

We nestled together in a house without enough room. We squeezed together around the tables or wherever we could find a place to sit. Eventually, after the enchiladas and rice had been eaten, the children ended up in the dining room playing table games and the adults gathered in the family room. Bob built a fire in the fireplace, and we prayed, sang, and talked. As we did, a phenomenon occurred that to myself I call the Shekinah glory.

Shekinah glory is a label some Jews and early Christians used to describe the visible approval of God. Its appearance said, "God is here. He approves of what you are doing," or as I might say, "God is beaming His approval." You could see the glory, observe it, know it was there, but you couldn't reach out and touch it, which might be why it was often described as a cloud. This is also why I was hesitant to share the label with others. *You saw what?*

There was no cloud in my family room that night, but there was a glow. People smiled and radiated pleasure. Emotional warmth was present and so was a sense of being connected. I could tell people felt closer to each other, closer to God, and sensed His presence.

No one else said anything, so I figured I might have been the only person to notice the glow, but I wasn't. Ruby and Thom moved again several months after that, and in December she sent me a Christmas card. She said she would never forget that snowy night at our house. She wrote, "I'll always remember the special glow that was present."

Affirmed that what I had seen was not a product of my imagination, I began to look for it in future celebrations. I noticed it was more likely to occur when we were in a circle.

The Circle Effect

I've always dreamed of having a really large round wooden pedestal table. My friend Charlotte has one, and no matter how many people are already at the table, there is always room for one more. A circle reaches out and draws people in. A circle gives everyone the same position—there are no levels, no one recognized above others, no one given the best seats. A circle makes everyone feel included. A circle facilitates focus, conversation, and interaction.

But even without a round table, I still try to maintain the "feel" of a circle. It is the way I think Jesus would entertain. I ask myself, *How can I bring people together and connect them? How can I make them feel close to each other, feel included in the activities, and feel at home?*

If we gather in the family room, then I arrange the chairs in a circle. If we dine together, we sit around our rectangular dining room table. It's not an ideal arrangement; I comfort myself by recalling that paintings show Jesus and the disciples sitting around a long, rectangular table at the Last Supper! Besides, if we hold hands in prayer, block out the world, and focus on meaning, we can create a circle effect. We can see each other's eyes; we can all converse together *if* the guests are cooperative. My husband and I try to keep the conversation going, but in any celebration, not all the variables are in the hands of the hosts. Such was the case when Steve, a friend of our son Joel, visited our home.

The Circle's Reach

Steve and Joel, high school band members, were very good percussionists who approached music with intensity and dedication. Steve was long, wiry, and a bit prickly, an independent boy who marched to his own drummer. His parents were separated, and Steve mostly took care of himself. He rode his bike everywhere, his unruly hair flying in the wind. He used his intellect selectively, which was not always pleasing to his teachers. He told me once, "I am not a student; I'm a learner." When he was ready to learn, when he found something that interested him, he pursued it with the same dedication and intensity with which he pursued music. If he considered a high school class fluffy or too elementary, he was not bothered by a low grade on his report card.

Either Steve considered social graces unimportant, or no one had introduced them to him. He barely responded to my overtures of friendliness; sometime he wouldn't even reply.

One morning when he got to our house early, I invited him to have breakfast with us. Ben and Bob ate quickly and went on their way. Steve, Joel, and I lingered at the table. Steve was talking, and when he paused, I made a comment. Without even looking at me, he said, "I was talking to Joel not you." I was stunned. As I could think of no appropriate response, I got up and began clearing the table. Steve had effectively shut me out.

It was a bit harder to be cordial to Steve after that, but Joel wanted to invite him to our Christmas party. I asked if he and Steve would play a musical number for us, as I was planning a Christmas carol theme for our party. They agreed and practiced "Little Drummer Boy" together on the marimba.

At the party—as we sat in a circle around the living room—the music of the evening stirred our emotions. At the end of our singing and their playing, I asked everyone to tell his or her favorite carol. I've learned that asking questions where everyone responds helps to achieve the "feel" of a circle. As we went around the room one by one, it filled with emotional warmth. The Shekinah glory descended and hovered over us while Bob closed with some devotional thoughts and a prayer. The guests stood up and started mingling and moving toward the kitchen where refreshments waited. Steve, though, came walking towards me with a quick, deliberate step. I didn't know what to expect. He grabbed me, put his arms around me, and pulled me toward him. It was an awkward hug, the gesture of an inexperienced hugger. He said to me, "Thank you." That was all, and I knew the circle had taken him in and warmed his heart.

My eyes moistened as I thought of a poem I had learned when I was a girl participating in a missions organization.

> He drew a circle that shut me out—
> Heretic, rebel, a thing to flout.
> But Love and I had the wit to win:
> We drew a circle that took him in!
> —Edwin Markham, "Outwitted," 1915

Chapter 18

THE POWER OF SHARED *W*ORDS

Bob and I were students in Texas when we became engaged. The first Christmas after he had given me a ring in the fall, we traveled back to the Midwest together. We went first to my parents' home in Illinois. He left me there along with his gift for me, then he went on to southeast Missouri to visit his mother. He planned to come back for Christmas Day when we would open gifts to each other.

I put the gift under the Christmas tree but it didn't stay there long. I was curious as to what it could be, not only because it was from Bob but because it was the most interesting package under the tree. The gift was wrapped in a beautiful foil paper of deep blues and greens with a dark blue bow that held a small bouquet of pinecones and evergreens. It was so beautiful on the outside, I just knew there was something beautiful on the inside—but what? I would pick it up, turn it around, and press on it, trying to figure out what it was. I couldn't shake it because it was solid and heavy, which added to my puzzlement. What could it be?

My mother, sisters, and I had several discussions about it. Naturally we connected the gift with our recent engagement. Surely it would be an expression of Bob's love for me, an expression that would be deeply personal. Or perhaps he was thinking ahead to our marriage and bought something for our home. Silverware. Now that would be heavy. Silverware. Surely that was it.

Christmas Day came and Bob returned from southeast Missouri. All day I anticipated opening the gift. When the time came, all eyes in the room—well, all eyes of the women—were upon me. I carefully undid the gift-wrapping, savoring the moment, to find...not silverware but a huge family Bible. I realize no Christian should say she was disappointed to get a Bible, but I was. I would have welcomed a nice study Bible or a Bible in a new translation, but this one was so big you could never hold it in your hands to read. It had numerous pages inside for recording family history, which is why Bob may have connected it with me, but I didn't make the connection. All I could see was a permanent dust collector!

I wish I could say that I graciously received his gift and concealed my disappointment, but I didn't. While I didn't say anything, Bob says I didn't need to. To this day, he can still describe the look of disappointment on my face. I couldn't help but be disappointed because I felt the gift did not live up to its wrapping. It was so beautiful on the outside that I expected something beautiful on the inside.

Have you ever noticed how we wrap Christmas to make it shiny and beautiful like Bob wrapped his gift? We spend time, effort, and money to create something that we look forward to opening. But sometimes when you open it, the inside doesn't live up to the outside. You expected to find something meaningful and satisfying, and it wasn't there. For me, this happens when words aren't expressed, and I'm talking more than greeting cards here! I need spoken words that will connect me with Jesus, with meaning, and with others.

Celebrating with Words

By definition, to celebrate is to hold up, to acclaim, or to extol what we value or who we are honoring. For those celebrating when Jesus was born, it was a natural response. They just had to say something!

After the shepherds saw Jesus in the manger, "they *spread the word* concerning what had been told them about this child, and all who heard it were amazed" (Luke 2:17–18 NIV).

When the wise men came to the house where Jesus was, "they bowed down and *worshiped* him" (Matthew 2:11 NIV).

The old man Simeon took the child Jesus "in his arms and *praised* God . . . The child's father and mother marveled at *what was said*" (Luke 2:28, 33 NIV).

When the prophetess Anna saw baby Jesus and realized who He was, she had to speak. "She *gave thanks* to God and *spoke* about the child to all who were looking forward to the redemption of Jerusalem" (Luke 2:38b NIV).

Words give us a chance to express how we feel about what we value or who we want to honor. Verbalizing what we are celebrating with others increases our joy and enhances the meaning. The meaning is magnified through shared words.

These verbal expressions can be spontaneous as those of the shepherds, Simeon, and Anna were. They didn't plan ahead; their words just naturally flowed.

In our celebration circles, we can have impromptu moments when someone tells a story, sings a song, or makes a comment that recognizes why we gather or what we hold in common. It can be said in a prayer when blessing a bountiful meal, or an expression of gratitude when opening gifts.

Often, though, in celebrations, we dress up our words, getting them ready for the occasion. We plan what we will say so the words will enhance or exalt the meaning. Often this is done in a festive or poetic way when celebrating. We would find this "dressing up" more in church services and community gatherings, but I like to plan for expressed words in my home gatherings too. I've found these expressions don't have to be long, complicated, or elaborate, just something simple to put the focus on meaning. It can be a prayer, a responsive reading, a brief testimony, a

Scripture verse, a story, a devotion, or even guided table talk. Words make meaning the centerpiece of the celebration.

Words also contribute to having spiritual encounters. Words of praise that extol and glorify God create a welcoming atmosphere. God inhabits the praise of His people (Psalm 22:3 KJV), so when we create a climate of praise we give Him a place to reveal Himself. In the circle of shared words, Jesus will appear and bless us with His presence.

Shared words not only connect us to God, but they connect us to each other too. Remember that it was through sharing answers to a question that Steve felt a part of our circle? Shared words bring warmth and encouragement to a celebration circle and help us feel closer to each other and to God.

Others may not agree with me that shared words are important to having a meaningful and satisfying Christmas. I realize I'm partial to celebrating with words.

Perhaps I'm partial because I'm a Martha. Martha was the talkative one of the Bethany sisters. The Scriptures do not record Mary saying very much. And yes, it does record Martha saying more than "Jesus, make my sister help me," as I will write about in chapter 23.

Or perhaps it is because I'm a writer and a speaker—a verbal specialist. I may look for—and need—words to be shared at celebrations more than other people who are not used to verbalizing concepts and feelings.

While being a Martha and a verbal specialist are both possibilities for explaining my partiality, I believe the main reason is because I've seen the power of shared words.

A Christmas Story

Seldom a Christmas goes by that my parents don't tell the story of a Christmas they experienced during World War II. Dad was sick and had been for some time, so he hadn't been able to work much. Sugar was rationed, so my mother wasn't able to make candy for her children and for gifts, something that was really important to her. Even though money was scarce, she was resourceful. For a Christmas tree, she cut a big branch off a lilac bush and brought it into the house. She took cotton and laid it in the limbs to make the tree look like it was covered with snow. She hung old ornaments on it and added tinsel and strung popcorn. But while she could produce a tree, she couldn't produce sugar.

She went to the store to buy groceries, knowing she would not be able to get any, but she hoped to get some hard Christmas candy for her children. Mother certainly didn't see any candy, so she asked the grocer, "Do you have any candy?" He answered firmly, "No, I don't."

She was so disappointed that she was pretty glum when she got back home. She grieved that in this dismal Christmas, her children wouldn't even have any candy. As she was unpacking the groceries, she couldn't believe her eyes. There in the bag were two pounds of candy! The stern grocer had hidden the candy in her sack as a gift. How Mother's spirit lifted as God blessed her and our family through a grocer's thoughtfulness.

My parents have gone through a lot more difficult things since that Christmas, and their grown children have too, but we never tire of hearing them tell this story. Afterwards we have the feeling that "God's in His heaven and all's right with the world." Our appreciation for our parents increases, our confidence in our fellow man is restored, and we are reminded of God's providential care.

As we sit at the table—where we usually are when the story is told—all around us will be evidence of how the Christmas was wrapped. There will be discarded tissue paper and bright bows, a punch bowl almost empty, stains on the tablecloth, and half-eaten pies—all signs of celebration, but that isn't what makes the Christmas good. It is when Mom and Dad tell their story. That's when the inside of Christmas is as good as the outside.

Chapter 19

I HEARD HER EXCLAIM AS WE *D*ROVE OUT OF SIGHT

The angel of the Lord and the heavenly host sang when they announced Jesus' birth to the shepherds (Luke 2:13–14). Believers have been singing about Jesus ever since.

Singing is a way we can actively celebrate Jesus' birth and verbalize what we believe in a poetic and emotional way. Singing can lift our spirits, fill us with joy, and give us words to express what we value and feel. As the authors of *Unplug the Christmas Machine*, Jo Robinson and Jean Staeheli, wrote, "Even if the tree, the presents, and the big turkey dinner were all taken away, it would still be Christmas—if you had Christmas music."

I agree, and the opportunities abound. We can sing in a cantata, harmonize around a piano, participate in worship services large and small, or stroll through the neighborhood singing Christmas carols. A Christmas caroling event is a good way to celebrate—it doesn't cost much money and all ages can participate. It is usually something that can be done without much trouble, or so I thought until I agreed to be chairperson of our church's Christmas caroling event.

A-Caroling We Will Go

I don't know which person suggested the idea of Christmas caroling for our women's group, but somehow I ended up in charge. At first I didn't mind. It would be just a few women and I looked forward to our blending our voices together, with some hot chocolate afterwards. Then we decided to invite our whole church to go along.

At this point, I was still assuming the job wouldn't be too demanding since our church is small and the women said, "We'll bring cookies for refreshments." I was thinking, *All I will have to do is make the hot chocolate.* Then one woman said, "Could we have coffee too? Hot chocolate has so many calories, and I don't want to overdo it this Christmas."

"Sure," I say with little enthusiasm, "I'll be glad to make coffee too."

Another woman said, "We ought to have punch. Some of the children might not like hot chocolate." So I needed to make hot chocolate, coffee, and punch. That meant finding a large container for the hot chocolate, having the coffee pot ready to go, and locating the church's punch bowl, besides buying all the ingredients. We needed cups for hot drinks and cold drinks, and then there were the napkins.

I asked, "Do we want the cookies served on napkins or small plates?"

"Plates. Definitely plates."

So I also needed plates and cups, which made me start thinking of the cleanup involved. *Oh, I hadn't thought of that.*

Joanne offered to lead the music, but she asked me if I would please select the songs we wanted to sing and have words available. Many people, she said, don't know the words to carols beyond the first few lines.

Again I said, "Sure," so in the next few days I selected carols and made photocopies for everyone. While stapling them together, I thought about the caroling and wondered if the evening would go more smoothly if we determined ahead of time where we would sing. I figured it would, so I compiled a list of names and addresses and planned a route.

As I thought over who would be in the list, I selected people who were lonely, particularly older people, people who had visited our church once, and people who were prospects for our church. One woman I included didn't live very far from our church. I put Mildred on the list because she was a widow who lived alone, and I suspected she had gotten her feelings hurt in the past at our church. I remembered seeing a crestfallen look on her face the day we mentioned a list of those invited to a baby shower; she was not on the list. She never came back to church after that. I called those we would carol to, including Mildred, and let them know we would be coming by.

Songs in the Night

The night we caroled, I tried to see that everyone got a song sheet as they arrived at the church. Naturally we had to wait for some people to arrive. As we waited around in the fellowship hall for those who lagged behind, some of the children ran wild. I tried to ignore them, but I have little patience for out-of-control kids. I figured they must have been on a sugar high from the Christmas parties at school that day.

Finally, when I thought everyone who was going to be there was there, I encouraged the participants to divide up and get into cars. Before we were out the church door, some of the song sheets landed on the floor. Others complained they hadn't gotten one. Some children didn't want to ride with their parents, and I suspect there were some parents who didn't want to ride with their children!

I couldn't believe how hard it was to get people in and out of our cars in an agreeable fashion at each of our destinations. It was like herding a bunch of cats.

Along the way, I heard complaints that this wasn't any fun. It was a cold night, so many people asked us in, which meant the children were distracted and tempted at each house. As the organizer, I felt responsible, so I had to keep a watchful eye on the children so that nothing would get broken. One preteen got mad and went home when we were near his house. And that's when, in true Martha fashion, I started counting the cost. Gritting my teeth, I vowed under my breath that I would never plan another caroling event. *Somebody else can do this next year.*

But Then...

My mood began to soften as I saw the reaction of the people we sang to. As we entered their small houses or their apartments, warmth entered with us. When we sang, people's eyes lighted up and smiles spread across their faces. I could tell their hearts were gladdened. Some, knowing we were coming, had refreshments waiting for us. They were glad to have company. Some mouthed the words of the carols with us, and others tapped their fingers or their toes. We were blessing them, and they were blessing us.

As my mood softened, I noticed other carolers were being affected too. The complaining stopped. Of course, having the cantankerous preteen exit the group might have been the reason, but I'd like to think it was the power of the music and the words, even if sometimes we sang off-key.

Mildred was the last one on our list because she lived near the church. The parking situation at her apartment complex was kind of odd. We had to park at the top of a hill and walk down to her apartment. She invited us into her tiny little apartment and announced, "I've never had anyone carol to me before."

Standing side by side and almost on top of each other, with our voices all warmed up from the evening's singing, we belted out, "Joy to the World" and "Hark the Herald Angels Sing." We were softer as we sang "Silent Night." As we filed out, we sang, "We wish you a Merry Christmas, We wish you a Merry Christmas..." That was all, but she thanked us profusely.

As we got to our cars at the top of the hill, I turned and looked back. She was still standing there, framed by the light of her open doorway. She waved and waved. I don't know if she saw me looking back or not, but at that moment she yelled out, "I'll never forget this."

Her words reverberated in my ear as we drove out of sight.

"I'll never forget this."

"I'll never forget this."

"I'll never forget this."

Oh, my, I thought. *So little. I did so little and it meant so much to a woman who had never had anyone sing Christmas carols to her before. And to think I had counted the cost! Shame on me.*

I heard someone else's words then even more clearly than Mildred's. It was Jesus speaking. I heard Him say, "Inasmuch as ye have done it unto one of the least of these...ye have done it unto me" (Matthew 25:40 KJV). I knew then I would be glad to organize a Christmas caroling event again. I would be glad to keep on planning, to keep on doing, because it is another way Martha can have a Mary Christmas.

Chapter 20

IF I HAD *B*EEN THERE...

O ne December Saturday, Bob and I visited some friends in another state. We arrived in the late afternoon and on our way into town, we noticed a new church had been built on top of a high hill near the edge of town. Thinking of Jesus' words, "A city built on a hill cannot be hid" (Matthew 5:14), I said to Bob, "What a perfect place for a church!"

Bob, looking at snow melting in the bright sunshine, said, "Oh, I don't know. How are the members going to get to church when it is snowy or icy?"

Later, over dinner, our friends said, "You must spend the night and go to church with us in the morning. You simply must see our new church."

I asked, "Does it sit on a high hill?"

"Why, yes, it does." Their new church was the one we had noticed on the way into town!

When we arrived at church the next morning, the hill was even steeper than I remembered. I could see

Bob's point about the difficulty of getting to church in bad weather.

When the pastor began his sermon, he said, "I have a story to tell you."

He explained how earlier in planning their new building, the church ordered a large cross to go on top. The cross was to be made out of fiberglass, so it wouldn't be heavy, but it would be bulky and therefore hard to ship. In order to save the church money in shipping charges, the manufacturer said he would ship the cross whenever there was room available on a truck. This made the arrival of the cross unpredictable.

Someone needed to be available to receive the cross. The pastor agreed to be that person and gave the manufacturer his phone number. The pastor said, "Well, the call came Friday night." Murmurs and chuckles rippled through the congregation. On Friday night, it had snowed. "It had been snowing a couple of hours and darkness was settling in when I received the call. The truck driver said, 'I have your cross. I must quickly unload it and be on my way. Where is the church? Can you meet me there right away?'

"I told him our church was located north of town right off the main highway. I said, 'You'll easily spot it because it sits on top of a high hill. I'll meet you at the bottom of the hill.'

"When I arrived, I got into the cab with the driver. He tried to drive the truck up the hill, but the steep hill was too slick from the fresh snow. We talked about what to do and decided to carry the cross since it was not heavy.

"I carried the small box of attachments and the truck driver carried the cross. It was taller than he was, and he hoisted it over his shoulder. It was snowing too hard to make conversation, so we walked in silence. In the fading daylight, I watched the driver ahead of me slip and stumble. The cross wasn't that heavy since it was made of fiberglass, but it was bulky and the road was slippery. Naturally I thought of Jesus and His walk to Calvary. I'll admit I had never really thought about what that walk must have been like for Him, but I did Friday night. I also wondered if the truck driver knew Him."

"When we reached the top of the hill and came into the church, I said to him, 'I know someone else who walked up a hill carrying a cross.'

"The truck driver said, 'Yes, I know Him too. I thought about Him all the way up the hill.'"

As the pastor went on with his sermon, I thought, *I would like an experience like that.* I had a hunch that an experience in which I could actually fall in step with Him would help me connect with Him. It's odd that I would say this because I was walking with Him—that's what being a Christian is all about—but I sensed that drama could heighten the experience and help me be more appreciative of Him and His effort on our behalf. Perhaps it was a desire like this that led St. Francis of Assisi to use drama to excite the inhabitants of a small Italian town to commemorate Jesus' birth with greater devotion.

The First Nativity Scene

Francis, who lived from 1181–1226, had a wealthy upbringing and gave up his riches in order to become a poor, itinerant preacher. His preaching and lifestyle included an appreciation of God's creation and love of all living things. When he felt the people had lost the real meaning of Christ's birth and that their celebrations had become too materialistic, he decided to put the spotlight back on Jesus.

He asked a friend who owned some wooded land to help him recreate that night in Bethlehem when Jesus was born. His friend agreed to do so, and together they set up the first nativity scene. They filled a real manger with straw, installed a life-sized figure of baby Jesus, and flanked the crib with living animals and people.

On Christmas Eve, Francis, carrying a lighted torch, led his followers and townspeople to the woods where the nativity scene was located. Before all their eyes was a stable, live animals, and a manger. With their senses fully alerted, "the glory of the Lord shone around about them."

Eager to make the gospel vivid, Francis preached. This man of God stood tearfully before the manger, full of devotion and radiant with joy, and spoke to the people about Jesus. So tender was he in his love for Jesus that he was unable to utter His name, so he referred to Him as the Babe of Bethlehem.

Up to this point the stories of this dramatic night agree, but they differ on what happened next. Some say Francis' message was so powerful that when the people looked into the manger, they saw the real Christ child.

Others say that the infant came to life in Francis' arms. Some say that miracles occurred and that even the hay, being preserved by the people, miraculously cured diseases of cattle, and other afflictions.

The truth among these stories is that *something happened*, even if we are not sure what. Something happened as a result of this dramatic evening. With their senses involved, they had a heightened experience of Jesus and His power.

More importantly, I think, for us than what really happened that night was the "catching on" of what Francis did. Ever since, believers have been dramatically portraying the birth of Jesus. They refresh their devotion to Him by connecting in a dramatic way with His birth. Today churches large and small have nativity scenes. Some are elaborate productions and others are simple. Some are well-planned and orchestrated; others are spontaneous.

Participating in a drama gives us a chance to picture another time, to touch and to reenact some of the mystery of Christ, and to connect with Him across the years. We answer questions in our minds: *What if I had been there? What would I have seen and heard? What would I have felt?*

I'm not partial to drama the way I am to words. I'm not an actress or a director, but I have been in just enough plays to know that what I am saying is true. And I have used drama informally enough to know it is a way to connect with Jesus. At parties, I've given guests a Bible with the sections in Luke and Matthew marked that tell the Christmas story, along with some costumes (bathrobes, towels, and old drapes), and sent them to another room to plan a presentation to give to the larger group. When they return, I see the light in their eyes and know they have put themselves back in time and profited by the experience. I am a speaker, and I've noticed that same kind of light coming to the eyes of listeners when I share dramatic stories that pull them in and make them feel part of the action. That's why I work at preparing talks that will make the stories of Jesus come alive.

Among the Splinters and Hay

I remember one late November when I was scheduled to talk to a women's group about keeping Christ in Christmas. That morning I decided I would take baby Jesus and the manger—the "authentic Bethlehem" one we were using with Ben—as a prop.

Around noon I borrowed some fresh straw from my neighbor and put it in the backseat of the car. Then I got busy with something else, and put off getting the manger out of the storage shed. The night was crisp and cool and the moon was shining brightly when I made my way to the shed and found the manger. Of course, it was dirty with cobwebs covering it, so I picked up an old rag, dusted off the manger, and hurried for the car. It was awkward trying to fit the manger in the trunk, and I got a splinter in my hand.

While driving to the meeting, the smell of the straw permeated the car. As I nursed my hand, I thought about how dirty the manger had been. Suddenly, it dawned on me how hard it must have been for Mary to give birth to her firstborn in a stable with smelly animals around. How hard it must have been for her to lay her precious newborn in a rough trough from which the animals ate. Joseph had probably cleaned out the feeding trough, but still...put a baby in a feeding trough? This is where they put the King of Glory! The lesson I had learned earlier about Jesus' becoming poor registered hard again. I started speaking with Him and told Him how much I appreciated His sacrifice and how my life was affected by what He did.

The message that night to the women flowed out of me, and the Shekinah glory was present. Afterwards I received comments like, "You were so radiant, as if you really believed what you were saying," "You made His birth seem so real," "I never realized it was quite like that." How could I tell them that it was due to a dramatic encounter when I connected with Jesus across the centuries? Maybe they would have understood if I had said, "On the way to church tonight I had a Mary Christmas!"

Chapter 21

RING OUT THE OLD, BRING IN SOME *New*

Anything repeated runs the risk of losing its meaning, and much is repeated at Christmas! "We always go to Aunt Sarah's for Christmas dinner." "We always open our gifts on Christmas Eve." "We wouldn't think of opening our gifts on Christmas Eve; it has to be Christmas morning." "Turkey is traditional at our house." "At our house we have standing rib roast."

We repeat what we emphasize. As with any holiday linked with meaning, we highlight every year the reason we celebrate.

The sense of "we always" can be very comforting and reassuring, but there can also be some subtle fallout that can affect our ability to have a Mary Christmas.

Our expectations are diminished because we know what we are going to do. It's also easy to stop thinking. The ceremony, the activities, and the festivities become the emphases, rather than tools meant to help connect with meaning.

We may begin to feel ho-hum about the story of Jesus' birth. After all, we heard it the year before, the year before that, and the year before that and.... Do I hear a yawn coming on? As one little boy at a Christmas pageant rehearsal said when he saw the familiar shepherd's costume, "You mean we're doing the same story we did last year?"

One pastor called it "spiritual cobwebs." He said, "Cobwebs are one of the persistent dangers of religious experience. When time and tradition erode the primary meaning of a spiritual symbol, when rite replaces reality, when shadows brush aside substance, when routine creates its own relic, cobwebs take over."

We Marthas know all about cleaning cobwebs from corners and ceilings, but I've found it more difficult to swipe away spiritual cobwebs. For one thing, they are harder to see! Instead of a gray, flimsy string waving in the draft, it is a shadowy thing in our spirit or a look of boredom or disinterest on the part of those we are celebrating with. Either is hard to gauge. For several years, when the boys were restless or sometimes acted disinterested, I thought maybe they were ready for a change. And yet the next Christmas they asked eagerly, "Are we going to do the candles again?" Eventually, there did come a time when they didn't ask, signaling that it was a time to change.

Christmas Joy Candles

When we were living in Stillwater, we began using candles to focus on Jesus' birth. A new friend introduced us to the Advent wreath—a tradition for some denominations, but not mine. Advent is a season of preparation, marked by the four Sundays before Christmas. An Advent wreath is a circle of greenery with five symbolic candles nestled within. On the first Sunday of Advent, one candle is lighted. On the second Sunday, two candles are lighted, on the third Sunday of Advent three candles are lighted, and on the Sunday before Christmas four candles are lighted. The fifth candle, the Christ candle, is lit on Christmas Eve or Christmas Day. Traditionally the colors of the candles are purple and pink.

Our friend suggested we let the first candle stand for the prophecy of Jesus' birth, the second one for the trip to Bethlehem, the third one for Jesus' birth, the fourth one for the shepherds, and the fifth one for the wise men. This way we could work through the story of Jesus' birth by candlelight.

I liked the idea of a candlelight ceremony, and I knew my sons would too. I stopped in my tracks, though, at the cost of an Advent wreath at the local florist. The florist did have a five-pronged chrome candleholder, though, for two dollars. My kind of price! So I departed from church tradition by not using an actual wreath, but I kept all the candle symbolism intact. I stuck some greenery in, around, and through the holder, and it gave the appearance of unifying the theme as a wreath would have.

Another change I made was to use red candles instead of the traditional purple and pink candles. The boys and I liked red. To us, red stood for joy, and it just seemed more appropriate for celebration.

Even with joyful hearts, I noticed the boys didn't get much from a brief candlelight service on Sunday. Just as I knew they would, they loved the candles. But they had little interest in the symbolism, Bible readings, and prayers that went with the candles. I wondered, should I give up or keep trying?

I chose to keep trying because they loved the candles and I loved the weekly emphasis. I wondered if varying the time of day might help. I tried after Sunday evening services, at the noon meal, and even in the middle of the afternoon. That was the year I called them in along with their friends from playing outside, served them hot chocolate, and lit the candles. Transitioning from soccer to spiritual meaning was too big of a jump! Gradually it occurred to me that perhaps Sunday was the problem. We were in church several hours on Sunday morning and two hours on Sunday evening. To add another worship service to our day, even if it was a brief one, was asking too much of children.

Saturday Night Special

One of the things I noticed about the brief services we did was the brevity of the candlelight. We lit the candles, had the brief service, and then blew them out. The candlelight just didn't last long enough. Thinking about that inspired me to have a candlelight meal on Saturday night. I used a cloth tablecloth, our best dishes, and glasses with stems. My children loved a dressed up meal—the kind we would have on birthdays and special occasions. They thought it was a big deal to drink out of glasses with stems. I wanted them to realize that Jesus' birth was a big deal, so I dressed the table accordingly. But this didn't mean that Martha was adding four more big meals to her Christmas list of responsibilities! Our Saturday evening menu of grilled cheese sandwiches or pizza didn't change. What changed was the atmosphere. Everything about the meal setting heightened their alertness and engaged their cooperation.

Bob gathered the boys to the dining table while I was in the kitchen putting the finishing touches on the food. They sang Christmas carols as I put the food on the table. When I was seated, Bob or one of the boys read the designated Scripture passage. We lit the appropriate candle or candles, Bob prayed, and we enjoyed the candlelight while we ate our meal. We really enjoyed this family time together, and the spiritual significance of what we were doing seemed to really sink in. This became a "must do" activity for us for several years, but eventually I sensed a need for change. This is when they stopped asking, "Are we going to do the candles again?"

Spiritual cobwebs had developed and we weren't consciously connecting with meaning; we were doing it just to be doing it. Besides, the boys were growing older, and I was feeling the need for another kind of connection.

Connecting Two Ways

By now Jim was in college, Joel was in high school, and Ben was in middle school. Our lives were more distinct than they had ever been, so I felt a need for us to connect with each other as well as connect with meaning. Keeping the glowing red candles, we dropped the weekly emphasis and lit the candles when everyone was home for Christmas. I asked each son to bring something that didn't cost money to the table to give to the others. Ben made a crude construction—er, I mean piece of artwork—of items he had found in the garage. Well, the items were free, and I had emphasized not spending any money! Joel played a drum solo. Jim read Scripture and an article by Andy Rooney. I shared a story from *Guideposts*, and Bob read a passage from the Bible that he had been meditating on. In between the giving of each gift, we sang a Christmas carol, and somewhere in there—I can't pinpoint the exact moment—the Shekinah glory appeared and hovered over us. Naturally, I wanted to repeat the experience, and we have many times.

Gathered in a circle at the table—even if it is a rectangular one—eating by candlelight and sharing with each other, we keep the meaning of Christmas alive and fresh.

Chapter 22

"DOESN'T THAT STRAW SPILL OUT ON THE CARPET?"

I 've always been amused by the book title *Happiness Is a Choice*, as if there's nothing to it except making one statement: I choose to be happy. Obviously, more is involved than a simple declaration!

More was involved for Mary, too, than a simple choice when she planted herself at Jesus' feet. Mary was a woman with a strong inner core who could ignore the criticisms of others and make the right choice.

Mary's Strength

To learn from Jesus, Mary ignored the usual duties of a woman, turned her head, looked toward Jesus, and listened to what He said. Mary had to know that her sister needed help, yet she deliberately looked away. Consequently, she encountered Martha's displeasure, evident in Martha's complaint to Jesus: "Lord, don't you care that my sister has left me to do all the work by myself? Tell her to come and help me!" (Luke 10:40).

Mary may have encountered the criticism of others present too. A woman being taught by a rabbi was scandalous behavior. It just wasn't done, but still she chose to sit at Jesus' feet.

Mary also encountered displeasure when she anointed Jesus for burial with very expensive perfume (John 12:3). The reaction of others who saw her, particularly Judas, was shocked astonishment at what they regarded as waste (John 12:4). The perfume could have been sold and the proceeds given to the poor. The other disciples did not rush to defend her. Only Jesus did. "Jesus said, 'Leave her alone! Why are you bothering her? She has done a fine and beautiful thing for me'" (Mark 14:6).

Mary wanted to be with Jesus so much, she was willing to encounter criticisms and defy expectations. I wanted the same thing as my love for Him grew, but this Martha had some inner growing to do.

Developing My Strength

To be independent enough to question how I celebrated and to make changes, to keep my Christmas simple enough so I could be spiritually sensitive, I needed a strong inner core. We spend a lifetime developing this inner core, but we can sometimes look to determine whether we are making progress. I'm glad to say I've made some progress since that Christmas when my dormant dream surfaced.

Staying focused became more challenging as life became more complicated. To prepare my heart-basket to be spiritually receptive through quiet times, learning, worship, and celebration required determination and discipline. I don't think any one thing helped me more with developing the inner resolve to having Mary Christmases than the manger my husband built, which I used to share the love of Jesus with our son Ben. The crudeness—and the oddity—of having a life-size manger in my living room took courage.

Minutes by the Manger

During the years I used the manger to teach Ben about Jesus and His love, I put the manger by the Christmas tree. I especially loved meditative moments, looking at the manger in the light from the tree when everyone else was asleep. Sometimes too, I would take a break from work in the middle of the afternoon and sit by the manger for a while until my breathing eased and I felt calmer.

Many a homemaker would not tolerate having a rustic feeding trough filled with straw in her living room. It is so "not Martha." Sometimes a visitor to our home would lift an eyebrow and ask, "Doesn't that straw spill out on the carpet?"

I would answer, "Yes, it does," and say no more. I knew what the visitor was thinking: *All the work that goes with the holidays, and this woman wants to add to it by picking up straw around a crude manger. What's wrong with her?*

Inwardly, I smile and cherish the knowledge that this crude manger with straw spilling out on the carpet connected me with Jesus, helped me deal with the pressures and expectations of the season, and enabled me to take a "Mary" stance. It put me in a position to hear from Him.

In our glorified Christmas card versions of Mary and Joseph, they are sparkling clean with a golden aura around them. They have the appearance of fantasy, so we are less apt to connect His birth to our lives.

That was then, and it was nice.

This is now, and it is different.

The two do not connect.

Those perfect depictions on Christmas cards give Jesus' birth a perfect, unreal quality in our minds. That crude manger in my living room reminds me that His coming was real. It lifts Jesus off the Christmas card and into 21st-century living.

Linking Then and Now

The season meant to honor Jesus often has the effect of crowding Him out. It demands so much. The "too muches" and the "not enoughs" take over. There is too much to do—shopping, baking, decorating, cleaning. There are too many gifts to buy. There are too many expectations to respond to. There are too many events to attend. There is too much food. Too much money is spent. While overindulgence is everywhere, the simple manger whispers, "Simplify, Brenda, simplify. Celebrate appropriately."

When the pressures of gift selection (Will she like what I bought?) and gift buying (How will I ever find the money?) close in on me, I sit for a while beside the manger. I reach out and touch the rough wood, and I remember the humble circumstances of Jesus' birth, and that He came to establish a spiritual kingdom. When I think about how I can spiritually give to others, I realize that money doesn't necessarily buy the best gifts. I can give of myself in friendship and ministry long after Christmas is over.

When I feel rushed and agitated by the expectations of Christmas, I think about how everyone had expectations of Jesus. He was courageously Himself, maintaining that His was a spiritual kingdom not a political one as the people wanted and expected. I remember what He said in a vexing conversation with the Pharisees and religious authorities. He said, "I Am Who I Am" (John 8:24, 28). He held firm and maintained His stance in the strength of knowing who He was. His words become my guide through the Christmas season. I am a woman who knows who she is; I am a Martha who wants a Mary Christmas. I am a woman who makes choices; I am a woman exercising some control over the kind of Christmas I have. I am a woman with limited worldly resources but with unlimited spiritual resources.

Sometimes when I move the manger to vacuum I get a splinter in my hand, reminding me that the first Christmas was not a perfect one, either. I become acutely aware that Mary and Joseph did not have a perfect place to lay their firstborn son. Jesus came into an imperfect world and accomplished His mission through imperfect people. That reminds me that my Christmas can be spiritual even when everything does not go perfectly or look perfect.

When I look at my home through the "company lens," I'm sometimes reluctant to entertain, even though I want to draw people into a circle of love. My furniture is shabby, the carpet is frayed, and the upholstery on the wingback chair has a big hole in it. I've tried covering it with an afghan and holding my breath that it won't slip off, but invariably it does, giving me a real appreciation for Jesus' words, "For there is nothing covered that will not be revealed." I cringe at the thought of specific, detail-noticing gazes of the Marthas who will come. When they step through the door, my house will be under their scrutiny. I think, *I just can't invite people to my home*, and then I look at the manger. I rub my hand over the coarse wood, and I remember Jesus will be present. I remember that He has given me everything that is really necessary to draw people into His circle of love.

So I breathe, "I am who I am," pick up my pen, and start addressing invitations. I start planning, igniting that "let's go" quality to celebration. My sense of expectancy increases as I look forward to hearing from Him. I can't predict when He will come and exactly how He will appear, but He will come. The Jesus of history will visit me in a fresh and unmistakable because He is who He is and I am who I am.

Chapter 23

MARTHA'S
GIFT OF *G*RACE

I was cleaning house, getting ready for Christmas, when a friend called. She wanted to know what I was doing.

I said, "I'm mopping my kitchen floor."

She said, "Don't you know that if you were really a woman who had it all together, you would have those floors already cleaned and you wouldn't have to be doing it right before Christmas?"

I gulped and stammered, "Well, yes, I guess you are right," and quickly changed the subject of conversation. How could I tell her that cleaning floors was a part of my Christmas giving? What person—or even what woman—would understand that? You may be puzzled, too, after what I've written regarding how much Marthas have to do at Christmas. I don't want to keep up with *all* the "have tos" and "you shoulds." I want a simple Christmas, but that doesn't mean I don't want to do anything. Being who I am is being a Martha, so even when I take a Mary stance, I still care about details and needs. I'm still interested in serving others.

Martha Was Still Martha

Jesus' rebuke of Martha when she complained did not mean that practical service was unimportant. Martha's service was important. Her home provided a place for Jesus—and perhaps His disciples—to visit and for Mary and Lazarus to live. Her invitation provided a place for Mary to learn at Jesus' feet.

In time, Martha got her chance to dialogue with Jesus, to learn from Him as Mary did. When Lazarus became ill, Mary and Martha sent a message to Jesus: "Lord, the one you love is sick" (John 11:3 NIV). They were certain Jesus would come right away and heal Lazarus, but He didn't. Lazarus died.

When Jesus arrived, Martha rushed out to greet Him, giving her time alone with Jesus. She said, "Lord, if you had been here, my brother would not have died" (John 11:21 NIV), but she was still confident Jesus could act. She added, "But I know that even now God will give you whatever you ask him for" (John 11:22).

Then Jesus encouraged her, "Your brother will rise again." Still expressing faith, Martha said, "I know he will rise again in the resurrection at the last day" (John 11:23–24 NIV).

In response to her receptive heart—her heart-basket was more than ready—Jesus made an astounding claim. He said, "I am the resurrection and the life. He who believes in me will live, even though he dies; and whoever lives and believes in me will never die" (John 11:25–26 NIV).

Jesus' claim was incredible—almost unbelievable. He asked Martha, "Do you believe this?" (John 11:26). She responded, "Yes, Lord, I believe that you are the Christ, the Son of God, who was to come into the world" (John 11:27 NIV)

Her statement as recorded in John's Gospel is like Peter's confession of faith recorded in Matthew and Mark. When Jesus asked His disciples, "Who do you say I am?" Peter answered, "You are the Christ, the Son of the living God" (Matthew 16:16 NIV; see also Mark 8:29). What insight on the part of Peter and Martha! One Bible scholar said Martha's words were an incredible confession that affirmed an incredible claim.

As remarkable as her faith was, though, Martha didn't stop being Martha. She still thought of others and noticed details. She returned to the house and told Mary, "The Teacher is here and is asking for you" (John 11:28).

Later, when Jesus, along with Martha and Mary and others, went to Lazarus' tomb, He commanded the men to roll back the stone over the mouth of the cave. Martha, with her keen sense of details, protested, "There will be a bad smell, Lord. He has been buried four days!" (John 11:39).

When Jesus returned to the Jerusalem area again for Passover, Martha helped serve the meal in

Bethany (John 12:2) at a celebration in His honor. Martha's serving provided Mary with another structured environment in which she could focus on Jesus, which she did by anointing Him with a very precious ointment and wiping His feet with her hair (John 12:3–8).

Martha was a woman of faith, but also a woman concerned about others and about details. Perhaps it was this concern that prompted the dialogue with Jesus. Thinking of Lazarus and thinking of Mary, she rushed out to meet Jesus for their sake. Because she cared, she learned from Him. She didn't have to stop being Martha to have a Mary experience, and neither do we.

Still Being Me

While I don't want to be encumbered with too much serving, I still want to serve. I do like a little urgency; it's a great impetus for getting things done. While I don't want to be responsible for *all* the details, I still find it necessary to look after some. Christmas wouldn't happen at my house without me, and I don't know that I want it to.

If someone else got my house ready, cleaned, decorated, bought all the gifts and wrapped them, purchased all the food and cooked it, and then said, "Okay, Brenda, celebrate," my celebration wouldn't be as rich or full. I agree with the family described in a *Guideposts* story that decided a sensible Christmas wasn't for them.

Every year, the mother, weary from cooking and housework, would say, "This is the last time I'm going to exhaust myself with all this holiday fuss. Next year we're going to have a sensible Christmas."

Finally one Christmas they did just that—no baking, no company, very few decorations, and a one-dollar-apiece gift exchange. They even went to a restaurant for a meal on Christmas Day to save Mother from having to cook, but by Christmas night, about the time they would usually head to the fridge for left-over turkey, they all regretted it. Being sensible snuffed the vitality right out of their celebration. In their efforts to be sensible, they lost the reason for Christmas, forgot about others and Jesus, and lost the joy. The next year they were back to baking cookies and getting ready for company!

When I'm cleaning, when I'm cooking, I anticipate what is ahead. A sense of expectancy develops about what is going to occur, and I look ahead to circles of warmth, love, and acceptance with meaning as the centerpiece. Feelings are stirred and deeper thinking takes place, all contributing to the heart-basket that I make ready for Jesus.

In the preparation and entertaining, I am doing what I do well. This is not an assessment in comparison with others, but a self-acknowledgement, part of that knowing who I am. If I can keep from putting on my "company lens," I enjoy preparing a nice meal, an open house, or a party for family and friends, and having a clean kitchen floor is part of the preparation! The work I do is my gift to others—a gift that I enjoy giving. This doesn't mean, though, that the gift will always be received graciously with appreciation, or even noticed. That's why I think of it as a gift of grace.

Martha's Grace Gift

Some recipients of my hospitality may never realize the work involved in getting ready for a meal they have thoroughly enjoyed. They don't always appreciate my preparation and attention to detail, which is why I think of my work as Martha's gift of grace. And to have the mindset to do this, I do it in the in the name of Jesus.

Jesus Himself did not come to be served, but to serve (Matthew 20:28), and so when I serve others I connect with Him. As I mop floors, clean showers, and make casseroles, I whisper, "Such as I am, such as I can do, I give in the name of Jesus."

With this attitude, I pad my heart-basket, giving Jesus the opportunity to speak to me, and He does. When I graciously do for others, Jesus graciously appears to me. Right in the busyness of cooking or cleaning, midnight clear moments come when I feel especially close to Jesus, gain a new insight about Him, or am alerted to ways He is working. I may be especially struck by how blessed I am. This may come while I'm on a ladder washing windows or have my hands in dishwater, but more often than not, those moments come when I am on my knees, mopping— when I am taking a Mary stance in a Martha kitchen.

Chapter 24

IT DOESN'T GET ANY *B*ETTER THAN THIS

Have you ever caught yourself thinking about the next Christmas as one Christmas is ending? Late in the evening on December 25 or driving to work on December 26, you take note of all your hard work, the frustrations involved, the things that went wrong, and you think, *Next year things are going to be different. Next year* you are going to plan ahead, start buying gifts in July, and have them all wrapped by Thanksgiving. *Next year* you will get all the decorations up by December 1. *Next year* you will have plenty of food in the freezer for unexpected drop-ins. You determine that *next year* you're not going to spend so much time working so you can enjoy your family and friends more. While you don't actually use the word, you determine that *next year* will be perfect.

Even as I learned to untangle expectations, simplify my Christmas, and pad my heart-basket, there was one remaining pressure that continued to haunt me. My ideal Christmas was one with lots of togetherness and a strong spiritual emphasis, but even when I was experiencing *Mary* Christmases, I also wanted Bob, Jim, Joel and Ben to have *Merry* Christmases. I wanted them to be satisfied, happy, and pleased with our celebration, and I worked hard to make it so.

For one thing, I always tried to spend the same amount on each child and also have the same number of gifts for each to open. When Jim earned enough to start buying gifts for the family, he tried to do the same thing. He walked in the door with two shopping bags full of packages and said, "This is ridiculous! Never again!"

"What?"

"I don't see how you had the time or energy to spend the same amount and give an equal amount of gifts. This is exhausting."

Expending that kind of effort to please my family meant there were a number of Christmases when I thought in terms of *next year*. If one of them even gave the slightest expression of being displeased, I would start thinking about *next year* and how I would do things differently. I don't know how long I would have continued this pattern if it had not been for a Christmas when I thought I had it right, but it was wrong for one son. That was the Christmas that set me free.

My Right Christmas

Christmas Day that year dawned early for the Poinsett family because we wanted to open our gifts and then get on the road. We were traveling to my parents' home for celebrating with extended family, about a four-hour trip. When we opened the drapes, we were delighted to see a winter wonderland. We had not expected the heavy snow that had fallen during the night. Not for a moment did we consider canceling our trip, but when we got out on the road, we noticed no other cars were out. The more we drove, the worse the roads became. We tried to get a report on road conditions from the local radio stations, but the broadcasts were prerecorded. Not knowing how far the bad roads extended, we decided to return home.

While I didn't say so, I was glad we were going to be home for Christmas Day. For the last few years I had wanted to stay home for Christmas Day. Ben was in his early teens, and I knew we wouldn't have many more years with all three sons at home. I never expressed my desire for this because I didn't want to disappoint our sons, whom I knew enjoyed going to Grandma's and seeing their cousins.

When we got back to the house, Ben went outside and chopped some wood, and Joel built a fire in the fireplace. I had some ham in the refrigerator, so I made scalloped potatoes and fixed some canned green beans for dinner. We sat by the fire in the early afternoon, played games, and talked—the picture of togetherness! Later, as the guys migrated toward the

TV and football, I took a walk alone in the snow and prayed and talked with Jesus, having a precious Mary time. I remember ending our conversation with, "Thank you, Jesus. What a good Christmas this has been!" But Ben, I was to discover, wasn't having the same kind of day.

Ben's Worst Christmas Ever

For supper, I sliced the rest of the ham for sandwiches and made potato soup. During the meal, Ben turned over his milk. I grabbed some dishtowels and tossed them to him. As he began wiping up the milk, he said, "This is the worst Christmas I have ever had."

Now those were piercing words for a people-pleasing Martha to hear. I excused myself, went to my bedroom, closed the door, and cried. Not a very mature response on my part; fortunately Ben's was better. After about 15 minutes, he knocked on my door and said, "Can we talk?"

Ben reviewed the day from his perspective. He didn't get to go to Grandmother's for Christmas, something he really enjoyed and had had been looking forward to. He broke the ax handle when he was chopping wood and felt really bad about that. While I was walking, he let his cat in the house, something that was against the rules. The cat made a mess in the house and Ben had to clean it up, not a very pleasant task on any day of the week, let alone Christmas. And then he was embarrassed when he overturned his milk.

He said, "I'm sorry if I made you cry. I didn't mean to. You know none of those things were your fault."

His words hung in the air as he went back to the family room. *None of those things were my fault,* but I had responded as if they were. Somehow I had seen myself in charge of all the variables that would give him and his brothers a Merry Christmas, but clearly I wasn't.

From the quiet of the bedroom, I could hear the sounds of living in other parts of the house. I could hear Joel in the family room stoking the fire in the fireplace; Ben was helping, and they were talking of plans for the next day. Jim was on the phone talking to a friend. The microwave was running, which meant Bob was probably fixing himself some hot chocolate. The thought occurred to me, "It doesn't get any better than this." Christmas is a mixture. It is a mixture of highs and lows, special moments and frustrating moments. Some Christmases will be better than others, but within any Christmas there will always be moments of the imperfect mixed in with the perfect, just as there were that first Christmas.

Glorious and Difficult

Things weren't perfect for Jesus' mother at the first Christmas. Rather, it was both glorious and difficult. How special she must have felt when the angel Gabriel appeared to her and told her she was chosen by God to conceive His son, yet that also meant being talked about in her hometown because she was unmarried and pregnant. Perhaps it was the town gossip that prompted her to go with Joseph to Bethlehem for the Roman census. She wasn't required to go. The Bible says that she was great with child; in other words, her condition was very obvious.

If I were great with child, I wouldn't have wanted to travel to Bethlehem on a donkey. I can only imagine how uncomfortable that would have been. And when I travel, I'm always ready for a good bed, but there were no beds for Mary and Joseph. An innkeeper rejected them, and Mary had to give birth to her firstborn in a stable, certainly not a well-scented area, and she had to put her newborn in a feeding trough.

The visitation of the shepherds was special. Oh, the stories they had to tell! But after they had gone and in the next few weeks, I'll bet she wished for family to see her baby. Fortunately, Simeon and Anna cooed like relatives over the baby, but even Simeon's praise was tempered with sobering words for Mary. He said, "A sword will pierce your heart."

Then the wise men came—that was a perfect moment when they recognized Jesus, gave Him gifts, and worshiped Him, but that too had its imperfect side. They had stopped at King Herod's on their way. Knowing about this child, King Herod put out a proclamation that all baby boys in the area under the age of two were to be killed. To save Jesus' life, Mary and Joseph had to flee to Egypt, where she knew no one. I wonder if she thought, "When I married this guy, I never dreamed I would have to go to Egypt. I want to go home to Nazareth."

In this mixture of perfect and imperfect, God was working. God never needs complete perfection to act. In fact, any less than ideal circumstances we experience may be the ideal time for Jesus to reveal Himself to us. A perfect Christmas is not required to have a Mary Christmas. Neither is it required for a Merry Christmas; when I realized that, *next year* became *this year*.

I gave up that earnest desire to make Christmas perfect for my family. I would still do my best, but they would be responsible for their own reactions. I could give, I could hope, and I could plan, but I couldn't control all the variables.

In the silence and darkness of my bedroom, with the noise of living all around me, I felt at peace with myself and contented, as if some big load had been lifted from my shoulder—and it had. I no longer had to make everyone happy at Christmas. They were free to be themselves, and I was free to be me.

Chapter 25

"OH, HONEY, THE *L*ORD SURELY SMILED ON US TODAY"

My friend June is definitely a "let's go" type of person. She could enter into anything with enthusiasm.

One day she and I were visiting in my living room when the phone rang. It was Ben, calling from the high school. "Mother, can you bring my swimsuit to school right away? I forgot it."

"When?"

"Now. Practice is right after school, remember?"

I looked at the clock. *Oh, dear. In just a few minutes, school will be letting out and the traffic flow will be horrendous.*

June, who also had a high schooler, was aware of the school's traffic problems. She said, "You get the swimsuit. I'll get the car ready."

I ran for the suit and June hurried out the door. I hopped in the car and off she drove. She let me out and kept the car running at the curb. I dashed into the school and handed the swimsuit to Ben.

I ran back to the car, and we took off like we had robbed a bank. When we pulled back into my driveway, we could hear the roar of the cars starting up in the school's parking lot. We beat them!

She and I both started laughing. I said, "I didn't know delivering a swimsuit could be so much fun." June made it fun because she fully entered the moment. She made Christmas meaningful in the same way.

True Volunteers Wanted

When June was in charge of planning a Christmas event for our Sunday school class's ministry to assisted living residents, she decided to have a live nativity, sans animals of course. Usually the class had Santa Claus appear, but this year June opted for a pageant of the nativity.

When she canvassed the class for participants, she said, "Who wants to help? I don't want anybody to do this who doesn't really want to. I want true volunteers."

June never planned for this to be a grand, well-rehearsed production. These were busy adults who would only have the hour on Sunday morning to give. She asked every volunteer to be responsible for his or her own costume. Someone would read the narrative from the Bible, so there would be no speaking parts except for the angel of the Lord.

June borrowed some props, including a wooden sheep, from a local florist. She asked Dave, her husband, to make a manger for her. He tore boards from their barn to build it. Susan had an unusual donkey-head mask, so she agreed to be the donkey.

June asked a friend with a three-month-old baby if she could use her baby for the pageant. Sharon said, "I will let them know that you are going to pick her up from the nursery. I will even have swaddling clothes for her. If the residents want to hold her, then let them." So that's how baby Jesus came to be played by a baby girl named Libby, a baby everyone wanted to see.

Let's Look at the Baby

With all this coming together unpracticed, things did not go smoothly (which we know doesn't really matter. God can still bless). Dave was supposed to bring the manger, the straw, and the sheep, plus his costume. He got there with everything but the sheep.

Ned, who was to be a shepherd, forgot to bring something for his head, so he used one of Libby's diapers to wrap around his head. Susan made a wonderful donkey with her crazy mask. She brought four huge brown fuzzy slippers for her feet. June's cape had pile lining in it, so she turned it inside out and threw it over Susan.

When the group finished the production, they sang "Silent Night" and mingled with the residents. They were so appreciative of the performance. June took Libby around, showing her to the people, letting some of them hold her. For some it had been years since they had seen a tiny baby, let alone touched and held one.

When it was time to get cleaned up and load the props for home, June laid Libby in the manger. It was filled with straw, and June had laid a piece of sheep-skin on top of the straw. Libby in her swaddling clothes snuggled in the sheepskin and went to sleep.

Like a magnet, the sleeping baby drew people to her. They gazed at her and said how beautiful she was. June was walking by when she saw a little old lady with a quivering hand reach out and pat the baby. She didn't know June was listening; she was in a world to herself. She said to the baby, "Oh, honey, the Lord has surely smiled on us today," and I believe He did.

Whether you call it the smile of God, the Shek-inah glory, or a midnight clear moment, when we open ourselves to God, when we prepare our heart-basket to receive Jesus, He will appear to us in a way so that we can discern His presence. When we choose to focus on Jesus at Christmas, simplify our celebration, acknowledge who He is, and worship Him, God is pleased.

My wish for you is—have the best Mary Christmas ever!

"*Can Martha Have a Mary Christmas?* gives us permission to simplify and focus on what truly matters during the holiday season. As sincere instigators of merriment, relaxing our Martha mentality will benefit us all. As a recovering Martha, I plan to take Brenda's advice and have a Mary Christmas."

—Jane Jarrell,
author of *Simple Hospitality* and co-author
of *The Frazzled Factor: Relief for Working Moms*

"In *Can Martha Have a Mary Christmas?*, Brenda Poinsett inspires us to slow down and smell the Christmas roses. Brenda shows us how to establish family traditions that focus on the babe in the manger rather than the bargains in the store. Like untangling a strand of Christmas lights, Brenda invites us to untangle the jumble of Christmas activities and simplify our lives in order have a Mary Christmas in a Martha world."

—Sharon Jaynes, vice president
of Proverbs 31 Ministries and
author of *Celebrating a Christ-centered Christmas*

"If you are having a hard time catching your breath during the Christmas holidays, Brenda's book can help you stop and inhale the refreshing celebration of Christ's arrival. There's no guilt trip about buying gifts or being too commercial; but she will help you discover new ways to connect with the heart of God that will satisfy your soul. The holiday rush doesn't have to squeeze out Christ. Brenda's stories and insights are the inspirational breeze we all need."

—Kim Wier,
director of Engaging Women Ministries
Author of *Are You Talking To Me?* humor devotional

"In this delightful book, Brenda Poinsett brings out the Mary in all of us as she provides practical ways to keep our focus on the true reason for the season!"

—Cyndy Salzmann,
author of several books including
Making Your Home a Haven and *The Occasional Cook.*

Also by
Brenda Poinsett

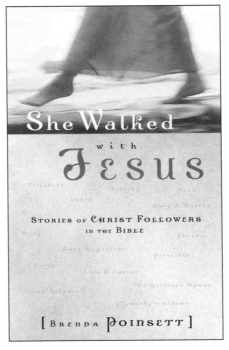

She Walked With Jesus
Stories of Christ Followers in the Bible

An intimate look at women who knew Jesus
and were transformed by His Grace.

1-56309-830-X

Available in Christian bookstores everywhere.